WHAT'S INSIDE?

INTRODUCTION

Histor y is Horrible. Far too horrible for adults to learn about. You see, people change as they get older. They get "civilised" … that means "soft". Now young people, they enjoy a bit of horror…

They love a bit of pain and suffering … as long as the sufferer is a teacher or the nasty grown-up next door who keeps your ball when it goes over the fence!

But adults try to protect poor children from horror stories. They put labels on films that say, "Not suitable for children". And they don't tell the whole truth about history.

So here's a chance for pupil power to strike back! Here is the *truth* about the Vikings. The things that teacher never tells you because teacher's too chicken-livered. Now you can watch Miss faint in fright as you describe some vicious Viking inventions ... for torture! See Sir swoon as you explain how Sigurd was killed ... by a *dead man*! This book is not suitable for adults. They will say things like, "Yeuch!" and "How sick!" And, when they do, just look sad and say, "It's true. But that's horrible history!"

VICIOUS VIKING INVADERS

The Vikings lived in Scandinavia – that's the posh word for Sweden, Denmark and Norway. The Saxons lived in England – they'd moved in when the Romans left.

All of a sudden, the Vikings started raiding Saxon England! And they weren't very nice about it. In fact they were pretty vicious! Lots of clever teachers will try to tell you why the Vikings suddenly crossed the cold North Sea and raided the suffering Saxons. But do they really know?

WANTED

Job: Pillagers. Brave, loyal men to work overseas

Qualifications: Must be ready and willing for adventure but not afraid to die

Hours: Long and hard (but a lot of excitement is to be had – would you rather stay at home and starve?)

Pay: Plunder – the more you steal the bigger your share. If you are lucky you could even end up in the Viking heaven of Valhalla!

Special note: This is an urgent vacancy – sailing tomorrow

Extra-special note: This post is not for the fainthearted

Apply within

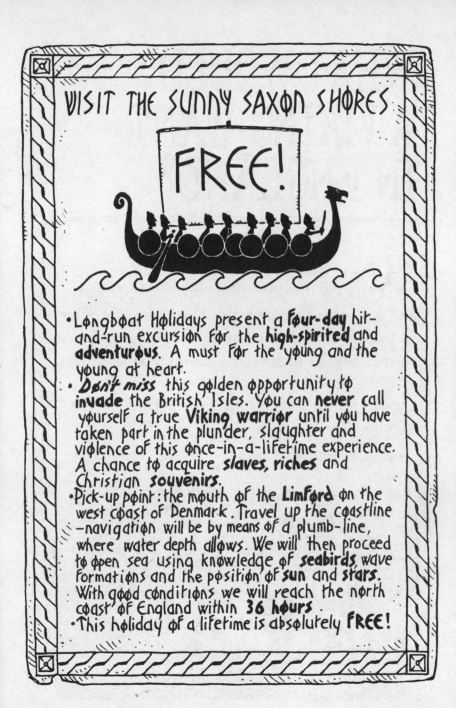

VISIT THE SUNNY SAXON SHORES

FREE!

- Longboat Holidays present a **four-day** hit-and-run excursion for the **high-spirited** and **adventurous**. A must for the young and the young at heart.
- **Don't miss** this golden opportunity to **invade** the British Isles. You can **never** call yourself a true **Viking warrior** until you have taken part in the plunder, slaughter and violence of this once-in-a-lifetime experience. A chance to acquire **slaves, riches** and Christian **souvenirs.**
- Pick-up point: the mouth of the **Limford** on the west coast of Denmark. Travel up the coastline –navigation will be by means of a plumb-line, where water depth allows. We will then proceed to open sea using knowledge of **seabirds**, wave formations and the position of **sun** and **stars.** With good conditions we will reach the north coast of England within **36 hours**.
- This holiday of a lifetime is absolutely **FREE!**

WHAT WOULD A VIKING WANT IN ENGLAND?

Work? Or adventure? What were the real reasons for the Viking invasions? Teachers and historians *should* be able to tell you, of course … but can they? Which of the following reasons do teachers and historians give for the Viking raids?

1 It was getting too *crowded* in Scandinavia – the Vikings wanted more land.

I'M SORRY BUT THAT'S ALL THE LAND WE'VE GOT LEFT

2 The monasteries were an easy way to *get rich quick* on treasure and slaves.

3 There was *too little food* in Scandinavia because the soil was useless – it hadn't been kept fertile with fertiliser because the Vikings didn't know about such things.

4 There was *too much food* being grown in Scandinavia – the Vikings needed to trade some of it.

5 Viking rules meant that younger sons got *no land* when their father died – they had to go overseas and pinch someone else's land.

6 Some pretty *vicious kings* took over in 9th-century Scandinavia – many Vikings sailed off to escape from them.

7 A change in climate made Scandinavia *cold and uncomfortable* – even wild, wet England was better than that.

SCANDINAVIA   ENGLAND

8 There was a sudden *shortage of herring* in the North Sea – their main food supply.

9 Sea trade was growing in the north of Europe – more trade meant more chances for *piracy* ... Viking piracy!

10 The Vikings *enjoyed sailing and fighting* better than staying home and farming.

The fact remains, the Vikings arrived. This is how it happened...

FEAST THE FAMILY
(AND GIVE FRIDA A BREAK) WITH

★ ERIK'S LITTLE VIKING MEAL ★

HERRING NUGGETS*,
BLUBBER, AND A FREE TOY

*Herring may not be included

TERRIBLE TIMELINES

VICIOUS VIKING TIMELINE

AD

787 Three boatloads
of Vikings land on
Dorset coast. A Saxon
tax officer orders
them to appear before
the Saxon king. The
Vikings kill him.
Perhaps they only
came to trade.

793 Whirlwinds, comets and fiery dragons seen in the sky over northern England. Bad signs. Sure enough, the first Viking attack on Lindisfarne Priory follows. Monks taken as slaves or thrown in the sea. Vikings go home for the winter.

VIKINGS BRAVE ENGLISH FROST

851 Vikings stay for the winter in England for the first time.

865 Vikings make first demand for Danegeld – in other words, "Pay us lots of money or we'll do nasty things to you!"

870 Vikings discover Iceland.

871 Alfred becomes King of Wessex. He batters the Vikings at Eddington. He rules the south and lets the Viking Danes rule the north of England.

878 Alfred defeats the Danish King Guthrum – they make peace.

886 Treaty of Chippenham divides England into two parts – Danelaw in the north – England in the south.

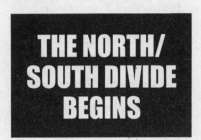

THE NORTH/SOUTH DIVIDE BEGINS

899 Alfred dies.

982 Erik the Red discovers Greenland.

986 Viking Bjarni spots America but doesn't land.

1000 Leif Erikson lands in America.

1013 Svein Forkbeard threatens to attack England. Ethelred, the English King, pays him off.

1017 Svein used the money to make an even bigger army. Svein dies and Viking Canute (Knut to his friends) becomes king of all of England.

1030 Christianity becomes religion for most of Norway after centuries of worshipping the gods of Norse legends.

1048 As if Viking attacks aren't enough, Derby and Worcester are hit by the worst earthquake in living memory.

1066 Viking Harald the Ruthless attacks York. English king Harold Godwinsson defeats him. But William of Normandy lands on the south coast of England. Harold Godwinsson rushes to meet him. William defeats Harold. Normans rule – end of the Viking age.

VICIOUS VIKING LEGENDS

You may think the stories you heard as a child were vicious – *Jack and the Beanstalk,* for example, where the poor old giant bashes his brains on the ground.

Or *Red Riding Hood*, where the wolf gobbles Granny before she pops out again when the woodcutter lops its head off.

Or that poor old witch in *Hansel and Gretel* who gets pushed into her own oven – all she wanted to do was eat the grotty little boy who'd been chomping her chocolate and nibbling her nougat.

But vicious Viking legends are even more disgusting! Viking story-tellers used to recite long poems, *sagas*, that told of disgusting deeds and horrible happenings.

GRUESOME GODS AND SHOCKING SAGAS

If you believe the poets who wrote the sagas then you'll believe the following…

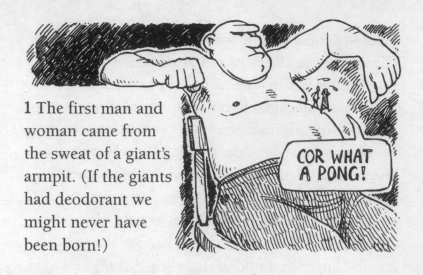

1 The first man and woman came from the sweat of a giant's armpit. (If the giants had deodorant we might never have been born!)

2 There was a huge flood in the early days of the world – just like Noah's flood in the Bible. But in the Viking story the flood was the blood of a dying Frost Giant. (Maybe that's why there's a Red Sea!)

3 Those aren't clouds you can see in the sky –they are the brains of a dead giant!

4 The sky is held up by four dwarves called North, South, East and West. You'd better hope their arms don't get tired!

5 If you die peacefully then you go to Hel. And Hel – unlike Hell – is very cold! If you want to go to Heaven then you'd better die in battle.

6 Some people were born to be slaves – the *thrall* class of people. They were ugly, stupid and clumsy but strong. The first thrall family had charming girls with names like Blob-nose, Oaf, Dumpy, Fat-thighs, Noisy, Servant and Bundle-of-Rags. The brothers were called Cattle-man, Hunch-backed, Ashen-face, Horse-fly, Shouter, Clott, Drott and Stinking. (And you have the nerve to complain because your parents called you Wayne or Deborah!)

BLOB-NOSE 'OAF' DUMPY DEBORAH FAT THIGHS

7 *You* might not believe in giant gods who rule the world but the Vikings did. Odin was the god of magic and war, poetry and wisdom. If you wanted him on your side then you'd have to make a sacrifice to him. At one sacrifice ceremony a traveller reported seeing dead dogs, horses and humans hanging from trees. There were over 70 bodies hanging side by side.

8 Statues of the god, Frey, usually showed him with no clothes on. When a Christian bishop saw one he was so shocked he took a hammer and smashed it.

9 Heroes who died went to a heaven called Valhalla. There, they fought all day and drank all night. If they were killed in a heavenly battle they came back to life in time to fight the next day. When they feasted they drank from the skulls of their enemies.

10 The Vikings converted to Christianity around the year 960 AD after a priest called Poppo performed a miracle. He held a red-hot piece of iron in his hand without burning himself. He said this proved Jesus was greater than all the Viking gods. King Harald agreed and became a Christian there and then.

In your childhood stories, the goodies always won. Cinderella lived happily ever after because she was sweet and kind. But in vicious Viking stories the *cruellest* usually won! And the craftiest! If the Vikings had told the Cinderella story then the Ugly Sisters would have married Prince Charming ... then murdered him and lived happily ever after in his palace. Cinderella would be one dead duck.

That's the sort of story the Vikings liked as they supped their mead and listened to the poets. And poets were very, very important people, as this story shows...

BLOOD, SPIT AND TEARS

"Spit in this jar," the great god, Odin, ordered. "Why should I?" the god, Thor, grumbled. He had a hammer and went around hitting people who argued with the gods.

"Don't argue, Thor, just do it," Odin sighed.

It would take too long to explain to thick Thor just what he was up to. "Look," he said, holding the jar under Thor's nose. "All the other gods have had a spit."

"Cor!" Thor said thoughtfully ... or Thor-tfully. "What you going to do with that lot, Odin?"

"Make a man," the chief god said.

"Oh, well, here goes," the hammer-horror shrugged and spat into the bowl.

And, using his great and godly magic, Odin made a man. He called him Kvasir and sent him down to Midgard – Earth.

Now Kvasir was the wisest man on Earth. (So would you be if you'd been made from the spit of gods.) He solved lots of problems for the people of Midgard.

Everybody loved Kvasir. Well, nearly everybody. There were two brothers, Fjalar and Galar, who absolutely hated him! Now Fjalar and Galar were mean, nasty and jealous of Kvasir. So would you be if you were a dwarf who lived underground with hundreds of other smelly dwarves. And Fjalar and Galar were dwarves.

"It is said that the blood of Kvasir is magical," Fjalar muttered one dark day … underground, all the days are dark.

"Is it?" Galar asked.

"It is. And we are going to get his blood," Fjalar chuckled.

"We are?"

"We are. Now this is the plan…"

"The plan?"

"We invite Kvasir to a party here…'

"A party?"

"Yes, you know, a booze-up. And when he's good and drunk you stab him!"

"You stab him?"

"No, *you* stab him," Fjalar hissed.

"What'll *you* be doing while *I* stab him?" Galar asked.

"I'll be waiting with those jars to catch the blood. Right?"

"Right!"

So the dastardly dwarves carried out their plot and bled Kvasir drier than a smoked pork pie.

The dreadful duo mixed the blood with honey and made it into honey wine – mead. And whoever drank the mead would become a poet and a wise man.

The trouble was, no one got to drink the mead. The bloodthirsty brothers kept it to themselves.

And as the years passed they grew crueller and crueller. One day they entertained the giant Gilling and his wife.

"He eats a lot," Fjalar grumbled.

"A lot," the gruesome Galar agreed.

"Let's get rid of him!"

"Get rid of him?"

"I say, Gilling," Fjalar cried. "How about some fresh sea air. It's getting stuffy in here! How about a sail in our boat?"

"Good idea," Giant Gilling growled. "You coming, Mrs Gilling?"

"You go, dear," Mrs Gilling grumbled. "I just get sea-sick. Have fun!"

But Giant Gilling had no fun. The deadly dwarves sailed out to sea and tipped him overboard.

"I can't s ... glug-glug-glug ... wim ... glug-glug ... specially with this stone round my ... glug ... neck! ... glug-glug ... I'm going to ... glug!"

"And that's the end of him!" Fjalar chuckled.

"And her?"

"We'll break the news. Perhaps she'll buzz off home," the devious dwarf muttered.

But Mrs Gilling didn't go. She just sat there and cried.

The giant tears fell on the floor and sloshed around the cave. "Me feet are sopping wet!" Fjalar fumed.

"Mine too."

"So get a large millstone and stand outside the cave," he told his brother. "When she steps out through the door just drop it on her head!"

Galar hurried to obey and Fjalar spoke to snivelling widow Gilling. "Just step outside and see the sea. I'll show you where your darling husband met his watery end … that's right … just step this way … no, after you. Right, Galar, drop it!"

Crunch!

"Cor! Stone the crows! It worked!" the brothers cheered. They went back to their cave and slept a happy sleep, until…

"Knock! Knock!"

"Who's there?"

"I'm Giant Sattung Gilling – looking for my mum and dad."

The giant boy was huge and wild and very, *very* angry.

"Your dad got drowned," wee Fjalar whimpered.

"With a great big millstone," gormless Galar grunted.

Sattung grabbed the two dwarves by the collar. "You tied a millstone around Dad's neck and threw him in the sea?"

The two dwarves tried to answer, give some explanation. But it's hard to talk when giant fingers wrap themselves around your neck.

Sattung marched into the sea. He walked for miles until the water almost came up to his chin. He dumped the dwarves down on a tiny rock. "The tide is out," he roared. "And when it rises up again you'll have to swim back home!"

"It's much too far!" fat Fjalar sobbed.

"Well, then, you'll have to drown … and serves you right," the giant orphan said and waded back to land.

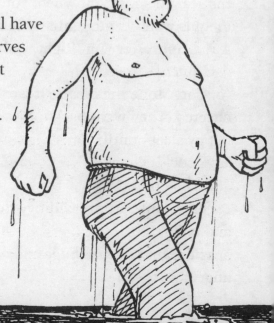

OI!
COME
BACK!

So Fjalar and his stupid brother lost the mead of poetry.

And *no one* ... not Kvasir, Giant Gilling, Mrs Gilling, Gilling Junior or the dwarves ... lived happily ever after. What a lovely story!

VICIOUS VIKING MYTHS

Myths, sagas and tales of the supernatural were common in Viking times. People believed that dwarves, giants and evil monsters were in constant battle with the gods. Stories ranged from the creation of the world, to its end, or *ragnarok*. Imagine a world in danger from demons and monsters, who at any time could create chaos and disorder!

Forget your warm and cosy houses, your televisions and computers. Gather round a blazing open fire, shut out the cold winter's night. It's story time Nordic style.

GOVERNMENT HEALTH WARNING

These stories are gruesome – if you suffer from nightmares then don't read them in the dark – you'll strain your eyes for a start!

Bedtime story no. 1

Once upon a time there was a god called Loki. Loki was an evil god who caused a lot of trouble amongst the other gods. He was an absolute nuisance (just like your brother or sister); very jealous and spiteful. Such was his cheek that he once wagered his head in a bet with Brokk the dwarf.

Loki lost the bet, but to save his life he pointed out that there had been no mention of his neck in the bet. Brokk couldn't take Loki's head without harming that neck!

Knowing just how bad-tempered dwarves could be, Loki should have known better than to cheat them.

But they got their revenge. How? By sewing his lips together! Moral of the tale: if you want to shut the school bully up – get the help of a dwarf.

But the story doesn't end there. This little incident did not stop the mischievous Loki. He gave blind Hod (the son of chief god, Odin) a piece of mistletoe to poison him. Hod, unable to see, took the mistletoe and died.

But the gods decided to punish Loki forever, so they tied him to a tree trunk and left him there.

Bedtime story no. 2

Thor was the god of strength and hard work. He was also the god of storms. People believed that he made thunder by riding across the skies in his chariot. Thor was also the protector of all the gods, and what did he use to protect them? A hammer.

Now Thor and his hammer were very close; so close that they never parted. He was so fond of it that he actually gave it a name: Mjolldir.

But one day (and what a day it must have been) he awoke to find his hammer GONE! It had been stolen by the arch enemies of the gods, the *GIANTS*! The only way Thor could get back his hammer was if he could persuade Freyja (the goddess of love) to marry the lord of the giants.

Freyja was desperate for a husband … but not *that* desperate. She refused. Now what would Thor do to get his beloved hammer back?

Well, he pretended to be Freyja to fool the giants. He dressed himself up in a wedding gown and

wore her distinctive gold necklace. Unfortunately, Thor was very manly … he had a beard and absolutely huge muscles, but *this* didn't give him away! What did? Well, at the feast he ate rather like a *pig*. Yes, Thor put away…

- eight whole salmon
- one whole ox
- washed down with three *barrels* of mead!

After this show, Thor's hammer was brought into the feast to bless the bride. Thor could restrain himself no longer, he jumped up to say hello to his best friend. His disguise fell off and he screamed, "I want my hammer back!" After a fight, the big soft lump got his hammer back, never to lose it again.

There are two lessons to be learned from this story. If you meet a Norse god…

1 Don't ask him to dinner

2 Don't steal his favourite toy

VICIOUS VIKING TIMES

Some people get upset if you say the Vikings were vicious. They argue that the Vikings were a cuddly, loveable people who were really quite clever.

For example, did you know that Vikings were great inventors? It's true! They liked to invent new ways for people to die! They lived in pretty vicious times.

Can you match the following people to their sticky ends?

1 King Edmund didn't want to fight against the Vikings in 869 AD. He wanted to talk to the Viking leader and convert him to Christianity. The Viking leader wanted to stick to the worship of Odin, so King Edmund was…

2 An English woman made a wax model of her hated neighbour and stuck an iron pin through its heart. She was accused of being a witch in 900. The accused woman was…

3 King Edward was assassinated by the servants of his own mother. She wanted her younger son, Athelred, to become king in 978. King Edward arrived to visit his mother without a bodyguard and he was…

4 In 997 King Kenneth of Scotland wanted his son to be king after he died. The other Scottish nobles didn't like this idea. Kenneth was lured to a castle where he was feasted and given lots of wine, then he was…

5 In 1012 the Archbishop of Canterbury, Alfheah, was captured by the Danish Viking invaders. They asked for a ransom of silver. Alfheah refused to let his friends pay a ransom, so he was …

6 The Irish King, Brian Boru, was killed while he prayed in a wood. The killer, the Viking Brodir, was captured and he was …

---

a) Stabbed. Had one foot twisted in the stirrup of a horse's saddle. The horse was sent charging off, dragging the victim to a bumpy death.

b) Taken to a room with a booby-trapped statue. When the statue was touched, several hidden crossbows were set off. The victim died in a hail of bolts.

36

c) Beaten. Tied to a tree and shot full of arrows. Cut down and cut up! Beheaded. Had head and body thrown into a wood.

d) Pelted with cattle bones and finished off with a single blow from an axe.

e) Drowned in the River Thames at London Bridge.

f) Cut open. The victim's intestines were attached to an oak tree and the victim led around the tree as the intestines unwound.

Answers:* 1c 2e 3a 4b 5d 6f

* Be careful! The Viking sagas were written a long time after the events happened. They may not be true. And the Vikings may have made up stories about terrible tortures in order to make them sound more brave and fierce than they really were!

The Saxon historians simply said of Edmund's death, *"and they killed the king."* They don't mention horrible tortures. What do you think?

But one of the unluckiest Vikings was Sigurd the powerful. He was killed by a dead man! Sigurd killed the man in battle, cut off his head and threw it over his saddle as a trophy. But the tooth of the dead man's skull scratched Sigurd's leg. The scratch became infected ... and Sigurd died!

(GENUINE) ANCIENT ENGLISH JOKE

When monks weren't writing books they were writing riddles like this one:

(No wonder you don't see many laughing monks with jokes like that! And no wonder the Vikings wanted to exterminate them!)

VICIOUS VIKING MEDICINE

L eif Erikson was probably the first European to land in America – so *there*, Columbus!

LOOK WHAT I GOT FROM THOSE FUNNY INDIANS

The Vikings called it Vinland – maybe because they found wild grapes on "vines" – Vine-land, get it? Or maybe it was because there's a Norse word, *"vin"*, meaning "pasture".

Leif left and told his brother, Thorvald, of the discovery. Thorvald and a crew of 35 reached the shores of Vinland (Newfoundland) in the

Spring of 1004. After making winter camp they ventured forth, first sailing east then north along the coast.

Thorvald and his crew met native American Indians. The Vikings called them the "Skraelings". During a major battle with the Skraelings, Thorvald was wounded by an arrow in the stomach. What happened next?

Did his men:
a) call an ambulance?
b) put him out of his misery?
c) try a little bit of Viking first-aid?

Answers: c) This is what Thorvald's men did…

VICIOUS VIKING FIRST-AID BOOK

CHAPTER 71
~AN ARROW IN THE GUT~

1 Cover victim with a cloak to keep
  him warm and comfortable

2 Give him this special meal : mix
  porridge oats with onions and
  herbs, then feed to the patient,
  forcibly if necessary

3 Wait until the food is digested

4 Smell the open wound. If it smells
  of onions and herbs, the intestines
  have been pierced and the victim
  will die. If not, patch him up.

5 Contact Odin, the father of all
  gods, and prepare the Viking for
  Valhalla (heaven, remember?)

By the way ... Thorvald died.

41

VICIOUS VIKING VESSELS

The Vikings couldn't have carried out those raids on England – and Ireland – if they hadn't been great sailors and built superb boats. They went still further – to Iceland, Greenland and even North America.

The Viking ships are admired for their low, sleek look. But they weren't always like that. The story goes that one man bravely changed the shape of the Viking longboat. This is supposed to be a true story...

ONE DAY A KING CAME TO INSPECT HIS NEW SHIP

WHAT A MESS!

THERE WERE DEEP NOTCHES IN THE GUNWALE OF THE SHIP

WHO MADE THESE CHIPS ?!!

I D-D-DUNNO YOUR HIGHNESS. I DON'T LIKE CHIPS

WHOEVER DID WILL LOSE HIS HEAD!

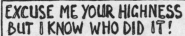

BUILD A LONGBOAT

1 Choose a spot near the sea.[1]

2 Choose your trees … watch the way they grow so you pick the ones that give the shapes you need.[2]

3 Pick straight oak trees for the keel – the backbone of the ship.[3]

4 Cut down a few dozen pine trees for the planks and split the trunks into planks by hammering in wedges.[4]

5 Drill holes in the planks to take the nails.[5]

FELLING TREES
@#!!
DRILLING HOLES
RIBS
OAK KEEL

1 Well you wouldn't want to carry the boat fifty miles to the sea when it's finished, would you?
2 Trees can take hundreds of years to grow. It's better if you don't spend hundreds of years watching them.
3 Oaks are getting rare. Cut one down in modern Britain and you may end up in jail.
4 No, you can't use electric saws because they haven't been invented.
5 And no electric drills either, you wimp!

6 Nail the planks so they overlap.[1]

7 Build "ribs" at right angles to the keel.[2]

8 Find a cow (or a sheep), and make ropes from the hair, dip the ropes in tar and pack the joins with the tarry rope and leave them to dry.[3]

9 Carve a really ugly face on the front.[4]

You're ready to fit the oars, the mast, the steering oar, and the sail.

Get a crew of muscular sailors and invade somebody!

1 If you ask a teacher to hold the nails then you won't hit your thumb.
2 They're called ribs because they look like, well, ribs.
3 This is messy. Do NOT wear your best clothes.
4 A picture of your teacher will give you something to copy from.

DID YOU KNOW...?

Ships carried tents and frames. The ends of each tent were carved with faces of fierce animals. These scared evil spirits away. The sailors could pitch the tents on the ship when they stopped for the night. But usually the sailors went ashore and snuggled into their leather sleeping bags … and sometimes they shared a sleeping bag to keep warm!

SHIPBOARD SNUGGLES!

BED DOWN IN THE HUDFAT, A COZY ANIMAL SKIN STITCHED TOGETHER ALONG THE SIDES.

Cuddle up in the spaces between each ship's thwart. **No farting!**

THE POWER OF VIKING POEMS

The first people to inhabit the British Isles were the battling Britons. Then along came the rotten Romans who drove the native British into the wet and western wildernesses of Wales. But the Romans went home in the fifth century AD to help defend the Roman Empire nearer home.

So the Angles, Saxons and Jutes moved in from northern Europe. You might have thought they'd be *glad* to find a deserted country to move into. But they were actually rather sad when they saw the ruined Roman towns: One of them wrote a poem called…

The ruin

How fearsome is this old wall,
Crushed and torn by time.
And great town buildings broken,
Work of giants dying.

Tumbling towers and fine roofs,
Broken down old gates.
Ceilings fallen, torn apart
By the hand of Fate.

Great bright inn and bath house,
Banquets in the hall
Once were filled with laughter.
Time put paid to all.

But 300 years later it was the Anglo-Saxons' turn to have their homes wrecked. By the Vikings. And those Vikings thought that poetry was pretty important too. One Viking even thought it could save his life. But did it…?

THE BEST POEM OF EGIL'S LIFE

Eric Bloodaxe was well named. He was king because he'd killed off all his rivals – including a few half-brothers. But he still had one deadly rival … Egil Skallagrimsson!

Then, in 949 AD, Eric Bloodaxe had the most pleasant shock of his murderous life. The doors of the royal hall in York opened and a breathless servant scuttled in.

"King Eric, your highness, you have a visitor, sire."

Queen Gunnhild looked icicles at the humble man and her voice grated, "Who is it? Speak up!"

"Er … he says he's Egil Skallagrimsson, your highness!"

The pale queen turned whiter than a rat's tooth. "Impossible. He wouldn't dare come here … not unless he has an army with him!"

"No, your highness – just a couple of servants!" the miserable man mumbled.

"Then have him killed!" the queen hissed.

"Yes, your highness," the man said with a bow that brushed the floor.

"No, don't!" King Eric ordered.

"No, your highness," the simpering servant snivelled.

The queen glared at her husband. "You've waited ten years for this chance!" she cried.

Eric nodded. "So another hour won't make any difference. I want to see this man."

Gunnhild rose to her feet. A spot of colour glowed in her frozen face. "Have you forgotten what Egil Skallagrimsson has done? Killed your friends and family – yes, killed your own son. He has scorned you and insulted your royal person. He has to die."

"Later," the king said calmly. "First let's hear what he has to say." He looked at a guard. "Have Egil Skallagrimsson brought before me," he ordered.

Egil was unarmed and half-smiling as he was led before the royal couple.

"I thought you were hiding in Iceland," Queen Gunnhild sneered. "What are you doing in England?"

"I came to see my friend Athelstan of the English," Egil answered quietly.

"Athelstan? Athelstan's been dead for ten years,"

Gunnhild gasped.

The prisoner shrugged. "So I've heard. But news travels slowly in Iceland."

"So you decided to pay us a visit instead," Eric Bloodaxe said.

"No. I decided to go back home. But a storm wrecked me on the coast not far from here," Egil explained.

"The gods will it. It is a punishment for your evil deeds," the queen said smugly.

"Perhaps," the prisoner agreed. "But I escaped the wreck. Perhaps the gods wanted me to live!"

"Or perhaps drowning is too quick for you," Gunnhild grated. "Perhaps they want you to have a nice slow death at the hands of Eric!"

"Eric is a Viking. He knows that fame is not bought cheaply. He would gain no fame from killing me now. If I'd tried to run from the shipwreck and hide like a common criminal, then Eric could have had me killed. But I came here freely, knowing Eric will treat me fairly. Then he will win word-fame."

Gunnhild began to speak but her husband silenced her with a wave of his hand. "Tonight I feast. Tomorrow I decide what to do with you. You may spend the night as my guest … in a cellar teeming with toads. Guards! Take him away."

And while Eric Bloodaxe feasted and slept, his enemy worked on his greatest art. His poetry.

The next morning the proud prisoner stood before the royal couple. "Your highness," he said boldly.

"Before you decide my fate, I ask you one favour."

"Kill him," Gunnhild groaned.

"No. Go on, Egil Skallagrimsson," Eric insisted.

"Allow me to recite a poem I have written to celebrate your fame. The people in this hall can hear it. My poem will bring you more than my death ever could. It will bring you word-fame."

"Kill him," Gunnhild shrilled.

"We will hear this poem," Eric said. "We can always kill him later."

And the court of King Eric gathered round the Icelander and listened. He chanted 20 verses he'd written in his head the night before. He began…

Listen, O king, what honour I bring;
Silence I ask while I play out my task.
Your brave deeds I'll tell, which all men know well.
Only Odin can say where the men you killed lay.

He went on to describe Eric's valour in battle…
Then Egil changed the rhyme pattern and made his
listeners wonder at his skill.

I praise this king in his own land,
I gladly sing of his just hand.
A hand so free with golden gains,
But strongly he can rule his Danes.

He finished…

To praise this lord, my dumb lips broke;
The words out-poured, my still tongue spoke.
From my poet's breast these words took wing,
Now all the rest may his praise sing.

There was a silence in the great royal hall when Egil
had finished. At last it was broken by one harsh
voice. "Kill him," Gunnhild said.

The Viking listeners muttered angrily. One spoke
boldly, "King Eric, this man's poem will bring you
word-fame. Your name will live forever. In return
you should grant him his life."

"Kill him," Gunnhild said.

"I will decide," Eric Bloodaxe said.

But what did Eric decide? Was the Viking love of word-fame so important? Or was his wife right – the Viking love of vengeance should come first?

In the end Eric decided that in return for the poem, Egil's life was spared. Egil's poem was typical of many. The Viking poems gloried in death and destruction. One poet wrote this to the gory glory of war...

I have held a sword and spear
When they were slippery with blood.
Hawks were hovering at the kill,
As brave the violent Vikings stood.

Red flames swallowed up men's roofs
As we raged and cut them down;
Bodies, skewered, lay there sleepy
In the gateways of the town.

But the Vikings didn't always win...

VICIOUS VIKINGS VANQUISHED

*S*omeone with a few brains could beat the Vikings.

Here are some battles the Vikings would rather forget…

The Wessex Star

A RIGHT RIVETING READ
April 871

YOUNG ROYAL LEADS ROUT AT READING

The Wessex Saxons washed their swords in Viking blood last night to celebrate a vital victory. And the surprise star of the battle was ex-king Athelwulf's youngest son, Alfred. Young Alfred showed big brother Athelred how to give the Danes a drubbing. The young Wessex Wonder was meant to lead half of the Saxon swordsmen, while Athelred was to lead the rest.

Imagine the popular prince's surprise when he went to King Athelred's tent and found his brother praying.

"There's a battle to be fought out there, brother!" Alf argued.

"I serve God first and men second," the crazy king replied.

So brave Alf decided to go it alone.

The Danes were favourites in the fight. They held the high ground. But Awesome Alf went at them "like a wild boar", one witness raved.

The bloody battle raged around a single stunted thorn bush. Saxons and Danes swapped places as both tried to hit that hilly height. At last the sword-swinging Saxons drove the desperate Danes back to their camp till darkness stopped the slaughter.

The Wessex Star says, "Move over, Athelred. Let's make Kid Alfred King Alfred!"

The Wessex Star's own poet wrote this ode to the great victory…

Ode to Alf who cuts Vikings in half

Our Alfie's the hero of Reading,

For he jumped like a flea from his bedding,

While King Athelred prayed

Good prince Alfred just slayed

Till the Danes were left bledding and dedding!

Note: Poor Athelred died soon after the Battle of Ashdown and young Alfred became King.

STILL ONLY
20 PENNIES

THE SAXON SUN

25 SEP
1066

A GOOD WIN, SON!

Heroic Harold Godwinsson has defeated the nasty Norwegians in the North of England. Yesterday, the Horrible Hardrada was stuffed at Stamford Bridge. Saxon England is free of those vile Vikings at last.

Godwinsson (known to his men as Gozza) admitted last night, "We had a bit of luck – but then, you need a bit of luck to beat the likes of Hardrada. The lads call him, Hard-as-nails Hardrada."

The "bit of luck" the great Godwinsson referred to was an incredible mistake made by hopeless Hardrada. The Norwegian ninny thought the Saxons were down in London, so he gave his men a bit of a holiday. One of the few Viking survivors described the scene to our reporter. "We was sunbathing, like. No armour – no nothing! Then we saw a cloud of dust and the sunshine on the spears. Well, we thought it was a bunch of our mates coming up from the ships, didn't we? I'd just turned over to tan the other side when they jumped on us! I couldn't find me trousers, never mind me sword. Sick as a parrot I was!"

The super Saxons tried to cross the river to get at Hardrada himself. A nutty Norwegian (a Berserker with a battleaxe) was on the bridge and battered a few of our brave lads. He also gave Hardrada time to warn his other warriors.

"Gave us a hard time," a Saxon survivor said. "Bit of a blood-bath, really. Hardrada asked Godwinsson for land but the boss just replied he'd give the Norwegian seven foot – enough for a grave … get it? Laugh? The lads nearly died … well, a lot of them did die, of course. But we won in the end."

Hardrada died in the fight. Now gutsy Godwinsson faces a new fight at the other end of the country. Our continental correspondent says that William of Normandy is planning an invasion on the south coast.

But *The Saxon Sun* says Harold will nobble the Normans in no time! That'll be one in the eye for William!

Editorial
The Saxon Sun Editor says…

Three cheers for brave Harold. He deserves an ode – so here's one what I wrote. We believe the people of England should sing this patriotic piece as he heads south to face William the Norman…

God save our gracious King
He done some real good things,
God save the King.
Send him a load of cash
As to the south he'll dash
To give old Willi-um a bash!
God save the king!

LIVE LIKE A VIKING

To understand history we have to try to understand the people who lived it. Can you get inside the mind of a Viking? Can you make the same decisions a Viking would have made…?

THINK LIKE A VIKING 1

980 AD Eiric's Story

Nothing is so sad as a beaten Viking. Nothing so mad. Nothing so dangerous!

Eiric was sad. To be beaten by the Norwegians in the battle of Hjorungavagr was bad enough. To be one of the 70 survivors was shameful. Eiric would rather have died in the battle. Instead he was a prisoner. Taken alive and tied with ropes to his comrades. The young man was mad…

"Why can't they give us a weapon and let us die fighting?" young Eiric cried.

The old warrior, Bjorn, next to him, looked at the boy wearily. "How old are you, Eiric?"

"Eighteen," Eiric answered.

"How did you live so long and be so stupid?"

Eiric's pale face turned red. "Why do you say that?"

"Because it is obvious, boy. They don't want us to die bravely. They want us to die as cowards. They want us to die pleading for our lives. They want to show that the Vikings are weak.

It makes the Norwegians look strong."

Eiric nodded. "But we will not die weakly. We will die as heroes."

"Better not to die at all," Bjorn sighed. "I've a wife and children who'll suffer when I'm dead. You've a mother and a father, haven't you?"

The young man turned his ice-blue eyes to the winter sky. "Yes," he said shortly.

"I don't fear death any more than the next Viking – but still it makes me sad to think of the ones we leave behind. Be brave … but be sad, young Eiric."

Eiric stared at the frozen ground and went silent while a flock of gulls screeched and circled overhead, sensing that death was in the Yuletide air. The young warrior struggled with the thick rope that bound him to Bjorn.

The old man shook his head. He chanted an old poem softly…

*It is frightful now
To look around
As a blood-red cloud
Shadows the sky*

The ropes were too strong. Eiric shook back his long, fair hair and said, "There is no shame in cheating death, then?"

"And how would you do that?" Bjorn asked tiredly.

Before his young friend could answer, the rope was tugged sharply and the line of captured Vikings was dragged to its feet.

Earl Hakon of Norway marched cheerfully down the line and called, "Does any man wish me to spare his life? All he has to do is ask, politely, and swear to become a slave to Norway!"

The Viking warriors stared at him with contempt. "Prepare to die," he sneered and nodded to a Norwegian soldier.

The first Viking was freed from the rope. He stepped forward, thrust his chin out and waited for the sweep of the sword. As his head was severed the Viking warriors cheered.

"Well died!" a huge warrior laughed and stepped forward to be executed. His hair was grey as the December sky. He turned to his comrades. "My friends!" he cried. "There is a better life after death!" He pulled a dagger from his belt. "When my head is off I will raise this dagger in the air."

He stretched out his arms and waited. As the sword fell ... so did the knife in the huge Viking's hand. The cheer this time was softer. Bjorn sighed.

Another brave man stepped forward. He too turned to the waiting men and spoke. "We will show them how a Viking dies! Executioner ...

strike me in the face. You will see that I do not turn pale!"

The sword fell. His face did not turn pale … but the Vikings saw that the man closed his eyes at the moment of death. The cheer this time was soft as the whisper of steel on ice.

Eiric jumped to his feet. He had to gamble on his plan to save the lives of the other 67 men. "Me next!"

When the Vikings saw their youngest step forward they struggled with the ropes and argued, "No! Me! No! Me!"

Sneering Hakon cried, "Kill the boy!"

"Wait!" Eiric said. "I do not want my hair to blunt your sword. Have one of your men hold my hair up while the sword falls on my neck."

The Norwegian Earl grinned and ordered a soldier to twist Eiric's long hair round his hands.

The Vikings fell silent. The swordsman raised his sword. The sword swept through the air like a longboat through the water.

At the last instant Eiric jerked back his head sharply. He dragged down the arms of the soldier who held his hair. Dragged them down into the path of the sword.

The soldier screamed as the steel bit into his wrists.

The Vikings roared.

Earl Hakon laughed. "Young man, for that entertainment you deserve to live. Set him free!"

Eiric's life was saved.

And so the story might have ended ... but this is a *Viking* story.

If you were a Viking, how would you want it to end?

a) Eiric goes home to his farm and lives a long and peaceful life.

b) Eiric refuses to accept the pardon unless the other Vikings are allowed to go free. Earl Hakon admires his bravery and all the remaining Vikings are spared.

c) Eiric refuses to accept the pardon unless the other Vikings are allowed to go free. Earl Hakon refuses and the boy is executed along with all the others.

Answer: b) The Vikings admired cunning as well as bravery. They liked to tell stories, like this one, where the cleverest Viking saves his comrades, while the bravest simply died. Of course, this saga may have been based on a true incident where a Viking army was defeated and executed … but the story of Eiric's trick is probably a story-teller's invention.

THINK LIKE
A VIKING 2

An old Viking poem gives advice on how to behave if you want to be a good Viking.

> *Do not laugh at the old and grey*
> *There may be wise things they have to say!*

(This doesn't apply to *teachers*. Vikings didn't have teachers so they wouldn't know.)

> *When a guest comes to your home*
> *Give them a wash and a seat nice and warm.*

(And never insist on showing them your holiday video or you'll bore the socks off them.)

> *Beer and mead are not that good,*
> *They make your brain as thick as mud.*

(And some people are as thick as mud even without beer and mead.)

> *A coward hides – at home he'll stay*
> *But time will kill him anyway!*

(But he'll still last longer than a warrior who goes out looking for a punch-up.)

> *A man who wants to kill his foe*
> *Must get up quick and never slow.*
> *A wolf that wants to have a snack*
> *Does not lie sleeping on his back.*

(Or… "Late to rise, late to bed, could make you healthy, wealthy and dead!" And this is why teachers get to school before their pupils.)

> *Cows and friends and parents die*
> *After some years so will I.*
> *One thing that will live the same*
> *Is a hero's famous name.*

(Not to mention the time you made a fool of yourself by being sick at your cousin's birthday party. Why do people never let you forget that?)

> *You never can tell who is out to get you;*
> *So look round a doorway before you step through.*

(And look *above* the door in case somebody's balanced a bucket of water over the top.)

> *When you go in the fields take your sword*
> *   and your spear;*
> *For some day an enemy just might appear.*

(This does not mean you have to take a weapon with you when you play football or hockey!)

THINK LIKE A VIKING 3

That same Viking poem gave another piece of advice. It said…

> *Even a handless man can herd sheep,*
> *But a corpse is no good to anyone.*

So, when they faced a fight they were sure to lose, they didn't waste their lives attacking. Instead they used trickery.

Hastein and his Vikings were probably the first to sail into the Mediterranean Sea. At last they found a great fortress of gleaming white marble…

70

The Luna massacre was a story told by an Italian historian, not a Viking. But modern historians think it's unlikely to have happened that way. By the time Hastein reached Luna in the ninth century, that city was in ruins anyway. And no Viking remains have ever been found there. Hastein *did* attack towns in the Mediterranean – but he never reached Rome.

VIKING GPS
(Global Pillaging System)

- ON A RAMPAGING RAID?
- WANT TO MAKE SURE YOU ARE PILLAGING THE RIGHT PLACE?
- SIMPLY LOAD UP OUR GPS, AND THE KEYS TO THE CITY CAN BE YOURS. THE RIGHT CITY.

ERIC THE RED

This is Your Life

TONIGHT WE HONOUR ONE OF THE GREATEST VIKINGS EVER TO SAIL THE OCEANS! EXPLORER, WARRIOR, SAILOR AND LOVING FATHER – YES! ERIC THE RED – THIS IS YOUR LIFE!

BORN IN SOUTH-WESTERN NORWAY YOU LEFT THERE AT A VERY EARLY AGE...

WE HAD TO LEAVE. IT WAS A SMALL MATTER OF A FEW LITTLE KILLINGS

DAD!

YOUR SON WAS BORN WITH RED HAIR

SO I DECIDED TO CALL HIM ERIC THE RED!

AT AN EARLY AGE ERIC, YOUR FAMILY MOVED TO NORTH-WESTERN ICELAND. A COLD, COLD PLACE!

BUT I KEPT MY DARLING ERIC WARM!

THJODHILD!

THAT'S RIGHT! ERIC THE RED – THIS IS YOUR WIFE! YOU HAD THE LOVING THJODHILD TO KEEP YOU WARM AT NIGHT

UNTIL SHE CONVERTED TO CHRISTIANITY – THEN SHE REFUSED TO SLEEP WITH ME

SORRY, MY LOVE, CHRISTIANS DON'T SLEEP WITH PAGANS!

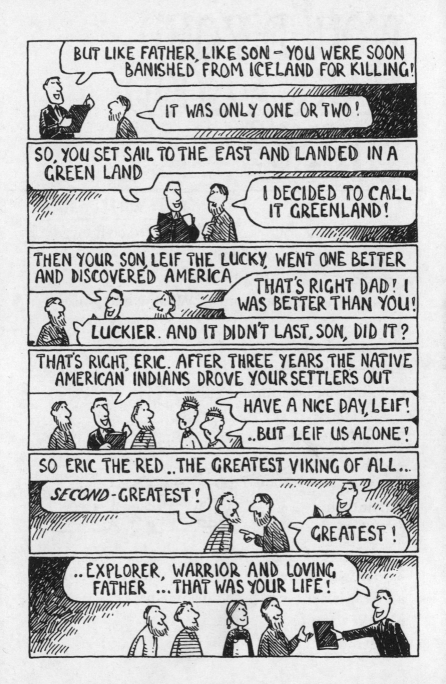

73

WOULD YOU MAKE A GOOD VIKING?

A nswer the following questions to see how good a Viking you would be…

1 You come home for a meal. What would you prefer?
a) A bag of crisps
b) Bread and cheese
c) Raw polar bear meat

2 Somebody calls your sister "Reindeer-face". What do you do?
a) Agree
b) Hit them
c) Kill them

HMM, HE MIGHT HAVE A POINT THERE

3 Your wife wears your trousers. What do you do?
a) Wear her dress to get your own back
b) Take them back
c) Divorce her

4 How would you like your bath?
a) Hot with foam
b) In cold water
c) In a steam bath until the dirt runs off with the sweat followed by a roll in deep snow

5 What is your favourite entertainment?
a) Reading a book
b) Listening to a good story – an exciting one with lots of fighting and dying
c) Picking a fight with someone and wrestling until you're exhausted

6 You go to a wedding. How long does it take you to enjoy your meal?
a) An hour
b) A day
c) A month

7 You go to a feast and drink strong ale and mead. When do you stop?
a) When you've had enough
b) When you're drunk
c) When you're totally unconscious

8 What is the most entertaining use for horses?

a) Pony trekking

b) Racing

c) Training them to fight one another to the death

9 What would you wear as you went into battle?

a) A bullet-proof vest under a suit of armour

b) A coat of chain mail and a helmet

c) Nothing except a small piece of animal skin to give you the strength of that animal

10 What would you use instead of toilet paper?

a) Yesterday's newspaper

b) Moss

c) Don't use anything

WHAT! NO MOSS!

HERE BUNNY BUNNY BUNNY

VIKING NAMES

Would you rather be an Orm, an Ulf or a Bjorn? Or may be even an Ulfbjorn? If so, you'd be named after an animal.

Orm is a snake
Ulf is a wolf
Bjorn is a bear

So you can work out for yourself what an *Ulfbjorn* was!

Vikings were named after gods – Thor was very popular. Many Viking names are still in use in Britain today – Rolf, Harold and Eric for example. But the great Vikings are known in history by their nicknames. For example, one king is known to us as Harold Fine-hair…

HAVE YOU SEEN THIS VIKING?

Missing husband. Answers to the name of Erik, when bothered. Tall, shaggy hair, unkempt, and grouchy. Check your sheds and outhouses. Approach with caution; **dangerously smelly**. Contact Helga. No reward, but not much for me, either.

HARRY'S HORRIBLE HAIR

The story goes that young Prince Harold fancied a beautiful princess called Gytha.

"Marry me," he begged.

But beautiful Gytha didn't fancy a poor young prince. "Ask me again when you have a proper kingdom to call your own."

Harold swore that he wouldn't cut or comb his hair until he'd made himself ruler of all of Norway. It took him ten years, but he succeeded. Imagine the state of his hair by then! But he won Gytha, so it was all worthwhile.

Then Harold went to the baths and had his hair trimmed, washed and combed. Everyone agreed that he had a fine head of hair. His name changed to Harold Fine-hair. Before, it was Harold Mop-hair!

What name would you give yourself or your friends … or your teachers?

TEST YOUR TEACHER...

Which of the following were *really* the names of Vikings?

True or False?

1. HARALD REDBEARD
2. OLAF THE STOUT
3. KON SMELLY-FEET
4. IVAR THE BONELESS
5. SVEIN FORKBEARD
6. ODIN PUDDING-FACE
7. HAROLD BLUETOOTH
8. KEITH FLATNOSE
9. OLAF THE PEACOCK
10. RAGNAR HAIRY BREECHES
11. SIGURD SNAKE-IN-THE-EYE
12. RUDOLPH THE RED-NOSE
13. SIGTRYGG SILK-BEARD
14. SIGRID THE AMBITIOUS
15. FLOKI RAVENS
16. ASGOT THE CLUMSY
17. GLUM
18. CONAN THE LIBRARIAN
19. SIGTRYGG ONE-EYE
20. THOROLF BUTTER

Several of these names belonged to very famous Vikings – Olaf the Stout and Ivar the Boneless, for example. Your teacher probably knows those. But, what teacher *doesn't* tell you ... because they don't *know* ... is that the Vikings *weren't* usually known by these nicknames when they were alive! The nicknames were usually invented by history writers in the Middle Ages to describe the different Vikings. So, it would *not* have been a good idea to go up to Viking Keith and say, "Good morning, Mr Flatnose!" The reply might have had something to do with the flattening of your own nose!

THERE GOES KEITH-REALLY-QUITE-A-NICE-NOSE-WHEN-YOU-LOOK-CLOSELY

WRITE LIKE A VIKING

1 Viking letters were known as Runes. Vikings scratched their runes on wood or stone. It's easier to scratch straight lines than curves. So runes were made up of straight lines.

2 The runes would be used by fortune-tellers who moved from village to village giving people horoscopes.

3 Fortune-tellers were so popular they always got the best food and drink!

4 Fortune-tellers like Kon deserved it. According to a sage...

> *The youthful Kon knew all the runes*
> *Runes everlasting, runes life-giving;*
> *Knew also how to save men's lives,*
> *Blunt the sword blades, calm the wild waves,*
> *Could understand the cries of birds;*
> *Could put out flames and quieten sorrows.*

5 Some historians say the rune alphabet was also used for magic. Charms, spells and curses would be written in runes. But the truth is they are only guessing this because some runes couldn't be understood! Most messages were simply everyday business, rather the way someone at home might leave you a message, such as "Don't forget to feed the stick insects" or "Your dinner's in the cat".

6 The rune alphabet was known as the *futhark*. But the order of the letters was quite different to our own alphabet, which is based on the Latin. We learn a-b-c-d-e, the Vikings learned f-u-th-a-r-k.

7 The Viking stories, sagas, weren't written in runes – they were memorised and recited by poets. They were finally written down 200 years after the Viking attacks had finished. They were written in Latin.

8 Twentieth century writers such as J R R Tolkien have used the idea of runes as a secret language. In his book, *The Hobbit*, the runes are the writing of the dwarves.

9 Some runic inscriptions can still be found on stones by the roadside in Scandinavia. They were written on all sorts of things found in the Viking household, because quill pens, ink and parchment (used by the monks in those days) were too expensive. The sort of things that have been found include:

"Kiss me" on a piece of bone.
"Odin" on a piece of human skull! A sacrifice perhaps?
The word *"kabr"* on a comb ... and *kabr* means comb!

10 Around the year 800 AD the runic alphabet was reduced to just 16 letters. This is very confusing for us because one letter can have several sounds – you just have to work out which! For example "u" rune can be read as u, oo, y, w, or o. No one knows why the alphabet was shortened in this way.

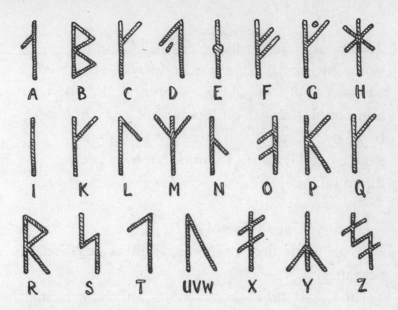

A B C D E F G H
I J K L M N O P Q
R S T UVW X Y Z

And here's a rune message … or it could be a rude message! What would this mean if it was written by a Saxon on a Viking wall…?

WASH LIKE A VIKING

If you decided to wash – and most Vikings did, once a week on a Saturday night – then you'd need some soap. You couldn't pop down to Boots the Chemist to buy some, though. You had to make it yourself. If you want to know what it was like then try this recipe...

Make your own Viking soap

1 Peel and mash up some conkers.

2 Add some water.

3 Squeeze out extra water.

4 Mould into the shape of soap.

5 Leave to dry.

6 Use as soap.

LOOK LIKE A VIKING

Maybe you'd like to look like a Viking. Perhaps you're off to a fancy dress party … perhaps you want to make a play about Vikings … or perhaps you just want to attack a monastery. (Take a bag of chips and then you can say, "Have a chip, monk!") Starting from the floor you'd dress like this…

SQUEAK!

Shoes: Vikings wore shoes of soft leather. But sometimes they left the fur of the animals on! Cover your own shoes with some furry material to give the same effect.

86

Trousers: can be narrow or baggy – the Vikings wore all sorts. Wear an old pair then wind strips of cloth up to the knee in a criss-cross pattern.

Kirtles (knee-length shirts): borrow a large, old shirt. Remove the collar or turn it inside the neck. Leave it hanging outside the trousers. Put a plain leather belt around the waist. (The Viking shirts were made of wool and could be dyed a single colour. They could be embroidered with silk or metal threads.)

Cloak: use a woollen blanket. Fasten at the neck with a brooch. (The Vikings used rough woollen cloaks and they also used animal skins. Wearing animal skins is considered cruel these days … so keep your hands off the neighbour's hamster – it would be too small anyway!)

Head gear: the Vikings wore long hair and long moustaches or neatly trimmed beards. (No. Not the women, stupid!) On their heads they wore hoods or fur caps. Of course, when they went into battle, they wore helmets.

VIKING WOMEN

GIRL POWER
- WE COOK,
- WE CLEAN,
- WE COMB.

Would you like to have lived in Viking times? And, if you did, would you like to have been a woman?

DID YOU KNOW...?

Viking women...

1 Managed the farms while their husbands were away – the chief would hand over his keys before he left.

2 Could marry at 12 – but 15 was more usual. Something very odd for those days was that a Viking woman could divorce her husband when she wanted to. One Viking woman divorced her husband because he showed too much bare chest.

THAT'S IT! OUT!

3 Would receive a bride-price (cash) from her husband which she kept. She also brought a cash present from her father – but got it back if they divorced.

4 Kept their own surnames after marriage.

5 Taught daughters to cook, milk cows, churn butter, make cheese, bake bread, brew beer, spin, weave, sew and skin animals – they also learned how to swim and use weapons in case they were attacked. Irish historians told stories of fighting female warriors, but they were probably untrue.

6 Could claim land. If a man came to a new country then he could have as much land as he could walk around in one day carrying a flaming torch with him. But, if a woman wanted land then she could have as much as she could walk around in a day leading a two-year-old cow.

7 Had names such as…

Sigrid	Thora	Ingrid	Gudrun
Tove	Ase	Ragnhild	Gunnhild

8 Were banned from longboat raids, but when the Vikings planned to settle a land they would take the women with them on the ships. Women didn't become merchants or craft-workers, but it wasn't all bad: there is a record of a Viking-woman who won fame as a travelling poet and another as a runecarver.

There is a story of the Red Maiden who was supposed to have been a warrior-princess in northeastern Ireland for a while, but it's unlikely to be true.

9 Were not treated as equal to men in death. While rich men were buried in their longboats, Viking women were often buried in a wagon instead of a coffin!

10 Had work which included combing her husband's hair … to get rid of the nits.

I SPOSE I'M AS READY AS I'LL EVER BE

THE BAD NEWS FOR VIKING WOMEN...

…the Viking tribes who settled in Russia adopted some of the strange and vicious funeral customs of the native people. The Arab traveller, Ibn Fadlan, described the funeral of a rich member of the Rus tribe.

Ibn Fadlan called this a "Viking" funeral. A lot of historians have said "this is how the Vikings treated their women". That's not true. All this bit of horrible history writing shows is how "Russian Vikings" treated *some* women. Ibn Fadlan wrote…

I'd heard a lot about the burial of the Rus Tribe chiefs and wanted to see one for myself. They burned the body in a ship, but that was nothing compared to what else went on! At last I was told of the death of an important man. Now was my chance to see for myself.

The man had several slave girls as wives. When he died his family asked the wives, "Who wants to go with him?"

One woman answered, "I do!"

When the day of the cremation arrived I went down to the river where his ship lay. I noticed they'd pulled it up on to the shore. Then they brought a bed and put it in the ship. They put a mattress on the bed covered with best Greek cloth.

Then along came an old woman who they called The Angel of Death! She's in charge of arranging everything and of killing the slave girl. She was a grim woman, stout and strong.

On the Friday afternoon they placed the dead man on the bed and covered it with a tent. Then they led the slave girl to a frame …

a bit like a door frame. She placed her feet on the hands of two men who lifted her up so she could see over the top of the frame. "What can you see?" they asked.

"I can see my master, sitting in Paradise. He is calling for me … let me go to him!"

So they took her to the ship. She slipped off the two bracelets she was wearing and gave them to the Angel of Death.

The Angel of Death led the girl into the tent. The men began to beat their shields with sticks so her cries would not be heard and upset the other women.

Then as the men strangled her, the Angel of Death plunged a knife into her heart.

The dead man's closest relative took a piece of lighted wood and set fire to a pile of wood beneath the ship. Flames swallowed everything – ship, tent, man and slave-girl.

A man turned to me and said, "You Arabs are stupid!"

"Why's that?" I asked.

"Because you bury your loved ones in the ground where the worms and insects eat them. But we burn them in an instant so they go straight to Paradise."

The idea of burning a body seemed to shock Ibn Fadlan more than the useless death of the slave-girl.

He also described a Rus custom of putting a favourite wife in a grave with a dead husband. The entrance to the grave is then blocked and the wife dies with him.

Today we are used to cremation but would be horrified at the idea of a woman giving up her life just because her husband died. BUT ... this custom wasn't recorded anywhere else in Viking writings, so perhaps it was more of a rotten Russian habit than a vicious Viking one!

TROUBLE WITH THE FAMILY

If you had a family then you fought to support it in Viking times. You also fought for friends, leaders and your in-laws. Everyone had so many friends and family that sooner or later they'd be involved in a "Blood Feud" – revenge taken by the shedding of blood.

The trouble was that taking revenge wasn't the end of it. The avenger would then have to be punished by his victim's family who would then be avenged by the avenger's family and … well, you get the idea!

Long-running feuds could only end when a referee was called in to judge what was to be done. Everyone agreed his decision would be accepted. He would then decide who had suffered the most and order the other family to pay blood-money. The payment of blood-money would even things up. There were no winners and no losers – honour was even and the feud could end.

Everybody needs good neighbours

How many points would you score in a family feud? You could score up to 10 points for common sense ... or 10 points for Viking sense! Which are *you*? Sane? Or Dane?

Your neighbour calls your mother a silly old bat. What do you do?

1 Agree with him and have a laugh?

Answer 1 Score:
common sense: 10
Viking sense: 0

2 Refuse to speak to him ever again?

Answer 2 Score:
common sense: 8
Viking sense: 2

3 Agree with him ... but kill him for the insult?

Answer 3 Score:
common sense: 0
Viking sense: 10

Your neighbour's brother kills your dad in revenge* What do you do?

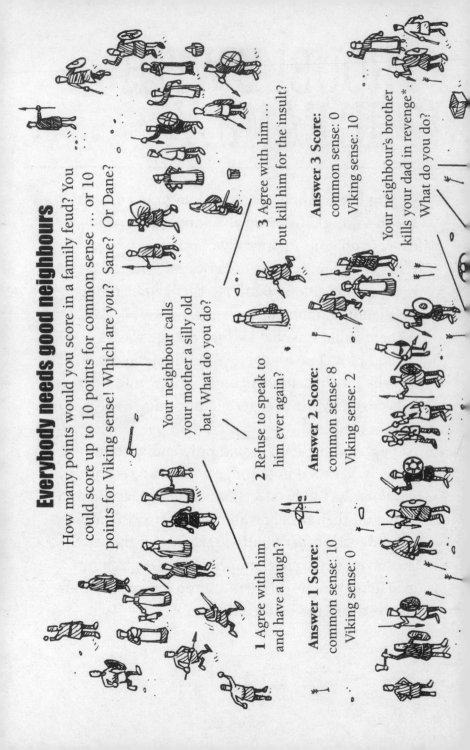

a) Demand "Blood Money" – cash for the life of your father?

Answer a) Score:
common sense: 2
Viking sense: 8

b) Call all of your family to fight all of the neighbour's family?

Answer b) Score:
common sense: 1
Viking sense: 9

c) Have a "Burn-in" – catch the neighbours at home, set fire to their house and give them a choice – die in the fire or come out and die by your swords?**

Answer: c) Score:
common sense: 0
Viking sense: 10

*When it came to revenge the avengers didn't always pick the killer – they often picked the most important member of the family … even if he had nothing whatever to do with the original crime or insult!!

**If you married into a feuding family you could choose whether or not you wanted to be part of the feud. A Viking woman who chose to die with her husband was Bergthora. Enemies set fire to her home in order to kill Njal, her husband, and her sons. They called to Bergthora to come outside and she would be spared. She came out and said, "When I married Njal I promised that we would share the same fate." Then she walked back inside to die with him.

Not all Viking women felt the same loyalty as Bergthora. Especially when their husbands had been bullies! Njal's best friend was Gunnar. And his wife had *quite* a different way of behaving when enemies came knocking on the door…

HALLGERD'S DIARY

My husband Gunnar was Trouble. That's right … with a capital "T". Whenever there was a fight in Bergthorshvoll then you could be sure Gunnar was in the middle of it. He was a bully and a troublemaker. Once – just once – he slapped me on the face. I couldn't hit him back. But I could wait for my revenge, couldn't I?

The day came when the council sentenced Gunnar to be exiled for three years. That meant he could leave Iceland, and live, or he could stay and the law would not stop his enemies from killing him. And believe me, Gunnar had enemies!

He decided to leave, but a strange thing happened. As he rode to the quay where his boat was moored, his horse stumbled.

LOOK DADDY!
AN ACROBAT

He fell over its head and landed on his feet ... facing the way he had come. He took one look back at his beloved farm and said, "Right! That's it! I'm not going." And he came back home.

Word got around and by nightfall the house was surrounded. Now, not even Gunnar could fight 100 men with his sword. But he *could* stay in the house and defend himself with his bow and arrows.

That's what he did. Until suddenly his bowstring snapped. "That's done it," he sighed. "I'm a dead man."

"Shame," I said.

Then he looked at me sort of funny. He reached out a hand and stroked my hair. "Lovely hair," he muttered.

"Thanks very much," I said. "It's not like you to pay me a compliment."

"I was just thinking. That hair would make me a wonderful new bowstring!"

"Would it?" I smiled.

"It would." He raised his knife. "Can I take a piece?"

"Remember the day you slapped my face?" I asked.

"What sort of answer is that?" he asked.

"It's the sort of answer that means 'NO'!" I told him.

"You shall not be asked again," he said. And he went out to die like a Viking. I'll say that for him. He died well.

But I'll say something else – and you men take note – he'll not be slapping me on the face again!

VIKING CHILDREN

Y ou may complain about Terrible Teachers and Pain-in-the-neck Parents. But life as a Viking child would have been harder than yours. For a start, childhood would have been short. The boys would begin raiding as soon as they were old enough and the girls would be farming and doing housework for most of their lives. Life was particularly horrible for the Viking slave classes – the thralls.

CHILDREN'S LESSON NO. 1

Don't get yourself born as a thrall!

A Viking writer described thralls as …

> *Wrinkled hands and knobbled knuckles,*
> *Fingers thick and face foul-looking,*
> *Back bowed down, and big flat feet.*

(Does that sound like anyone you know?)

GRAVEYARD QUEUE

A thrall's life was not a happy one. She/he had to work on the land to make a living, but she/he also had to work for a master for no pay! And what work!

A male slave would...

- build walls
- cover the fields with manure
- herd pigs and goats
- dig peat (a sort of turf burned for fuel)

A female slave would...

- grind corn by hand
- milk cows and goats
- make cheese
- cook
- wash

Thralls had to have their master's permission to get married. They couldn't go anywhere without permission. But a thrall could work hard and buy his freedom. Apart from freedom in life he even got a better *death*! The Christian laws of south-east Norway give an order for burying people in the graveyard...

- the freemen, their wives and children get the best spot – near the church
- then come the thralls and their families, further from the church
- lastly come the corpses washed ashore – so long as the corpse had a Norwegian hair-style. If it didn't then it was a foreigner – and it probably didn't get into the graveyard at all.

DID YOU KNOW...?

It was against the law to call a free-born man a "thrall" (a slave). The biggest disgrace was to die in a fight with a thrall.

ICELANDIC HOUSES

Children and women would spend more time at home than the men. This must have been especially hard if you lived in a Viking house in Iceland...

To keep out the cold the Vikings lived in houses built of turf. The walls were thick and the houses looked like little hills. The children could play on the roofs ... and keep the animals off, because the danger was that a hungry cow would climb up and eat through your roof.

The houses were pretty air-tight. The good news was that this kept out the cold. The bad news was that it also kept out the light and kept in the smoke from your fire. As your fuel may have been cattle-droppings then you had a choice – freeze outside or choke inside!

If you wanted a bath then you'd pop down to the bath house. It was what we'd call a "sauna" today. Water was poured over hot stones and you had a steam-clean. To really freshen up you'd whip yourself with twigs ... then run outside to roll in the snow. If you were a softie then you'd go along to one of Iceland's warm-water springs.

SVEN! YOU'RE SUPPOSED TO ROLL IN THE SNOW *AFTER* THE SAUNA

VIKING FUN

Of course, there were no schools. Children learned by working alongside their mothers and fathers. But there would be a little time for play. If you'd like to try a Viking game, then play...

Kingy bats

1 Take a circle of wood about 40 cm across.

2 Glue or staple a strap across the back so you can hold it like a shield. Each player needs one of these bats.

3 Make a ball out of rags bound up with string (about the size of a tennis ball).

4 Stand in a circle and pass the rag ball.

5 To make it a competition, split into pairs. The winners are the pair who can keep the ball in the air longest without letting it hit the ground.

• Other children's games included making up poems and riddles. An adult game, which children might have tried, included a type of chess.

And just as we have the shot put in today's athletics, the Vikings threw boulders. The furthest was the winner.

HE'S STRONGER THAN HE LOOKS

• Vikings made skates for crossing frozen rivers. The skates were made from bones, and poles were used to push the skaters along, rather like skiing today. The Vikings called their skates "ice-legs"!

A VIKING GAME YOU PROBABLY WOULDN'T WANT TO PLAY

P-pick up a Puffin

In Iceland today, a Viking descendant describes the national sports as gannet-egg-gathering and puffin hunting. They catch flying puffins in a net on the end of a pole then wring their necks and eat them roasted. 12,000 puffins a year die like this.

So now you know something about life for Viking warriors, women and children. Now amaze your friends, your parents and even your horrible history teachers with…

TEN THINGS YOU DIDN'T KNOW ABOUT THE VIKINGS

1 Early Vikings had no buttons – they used brooches. And their houses had no windows.

2 The Viking blacksmiths hardened their swords by cooling them quickly in water – or sometimes in blood!

3 The children's song, *London Bridge is Falling Down*, is about a Viking attack led by Olaf. English soldiers fired arrows from the bridge into Olaf's attacking longboats. So Olaf attached ropes to

the bridge's wooden legs and the other ends to his ships. The Vikings rowed away as fast as they could. Result … London Bridge was falling down!

4 If you made a sacrifice to the gods and wanted all your neighbours to know how good you were, then you'd put it on poles outside your front door!

5 Viking warriors could make close friends into "blood brothers" by cutting themselves and letting their blood mix. They often did the mixing under a circle of turf that had been lifted from the ground. Their blood mixed with the soil to make mud!

6 The Vikings made a promise by swearing an oath on a holy ring. This was a ring that was placed on an altar and reddened with the blood of a sacrificed animal.

7 One group of Vikings were reported to have a curious funeral custom. They split the dead man's possessions up and placed them in five or six portions. They placed these within a mile of the dead man's house. Then the men took their horses and raced to the piles. The first to get there won the dead man's loot!

8 The Vikings rarely took prisoners in sea battles because there was no room for them in the longboats. They let the losers drown or killed them.

9 No one was taken on board a longboat unless they had proved they were skilled with an oar, a sword and an axe.

10 Vikings shared their treasures evenly. You agreed what your share would be when you joined the longboat crew.

VILE VIKING FOOD

Would you like to eat a "cauldron snake"? Probably. It's the Viking name for a sausage spiced with thyme and garlic.

Summers were often short, cold and wet (just like Britain really!), whilst in winter it snowed from October to February. Crops had little time to grow, and poor harvests meant no food.

So Vikings either starved or … went hunting.

VIKING FOOD YOU MIGHT LIKE TO TRY...

Some of the food, like cheeses and smoked meats, needed no cooking. Bread was baked and meat roasted on a spit, or baked in a deep pit covered with hot stones. Sometimes it was boiled in an iron cauldron.

Food and soup was served in wooden bowls, and drink taken from cups made from the horns of animals such as reindeer. The Vikings used knives, fingers and sometimes very small spoons – but no forks.

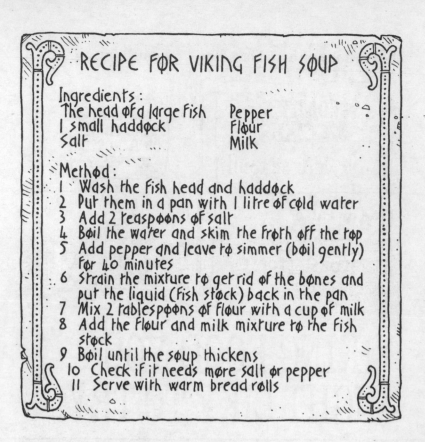

RECIPE FOR VIKING FISH SOUP

Ingredients:
The head of a large fish
1 small haddock
Salt
Pepper
Flour
Milk

Method:
1 Wash the fish head and haddock
2 Put them in a pan with 1 litre of cold water
3 Add 2 teaspoons of salt
4 Boil the water and skim the froth off the top
5 Add pepper and leave to simmer (boil gently) for 40 minutes
6 Strain the mixture to get rid of the bones and put the liquid (fish stock) back in the pan
7 Mix 2 tablespoons of flour with a cup of milk
8 Add the flour and milk mixture to the fish stock
9 Boil until the soup thickens
10 Check if it needs more salt or pepper
11 Serve with warm bread rolls

VILE VIKING JOKE

SOME VIKING FOODS YOU WOULDN'T WANT TO TRY...

True or False? The Vikings ate...

1 Easily netted and very tasty in Viking stew.

2 Nothing wasted, goose feathers were also used for bedding and quilts.

3 A great alternative to chicken and goose.

4 Skins used for clothing.

5 A wild version of today's pig.

6 Meat was eaten and the fur made into clothes or used for trade with other countries.

7 Waste not want not. Walrus ivory was in great demand from those in foreign countries.

8 Roaming through massive forests by the fjords, even moose weren't safe from the Vikings' bows. Their antlers were used as knife handles and hair combs.

116

9 The Vikings appear to have been the first whale hunters. It often took between 10 and 15 men to kill just one whale, all taking turns to spear the poor creature. A long and painful death for the whale, but to the Vikings the whale was the scourge of the sea, often overturning their ships, so it deserved to die.

10 Even the horses didn't escape the mighty Viking sword … yes, once the poor family nag was past it – chop!

The Vikings also enjoyed seaweed … the Welsh still eat it (but they call it lava bread) and it's considered a delicacy in Japanese restaurants.

During bad winters (most winters!) the Vikings ate anything they could catch, including foxes and ravens.

A VIKING YOU WOULDN'T WANT TO HAVE TEA WITH...

Harthacnut was Viking King of England from 1040 till 1042. He *could* have had a feast set out just once a day. If guests got hungry later, they *could* have eaten the leftovers. But Harthacnut wouldn't have this. When the guests had finished a feast he had the tables cleared of leftovers. Then another feast was set out. And after that another!

Every day he had FOUR feasts set out. Surprise, surprise – Harthacnut died young from eating and drinking too much.

WHAT DID VIKINGS DRINK?

Beer and mead were drunk from the horns of cattle. This was an art in itself- a trickle could soon become a tidal wave if the horn was tipped too far!

Another major problem was the horn's shape –
it couldn't be put down unless it was empty. The
drink had to be drunk in one go, hence a drunken
Viking was a common sight.

VIKING BREAD...
OR, TEETH DON'T
GROW ON TREES!

When food was scarce, Viking women made
bread with flour, peas and pine-tree bark
(for roughage and for vitamin C).

This, as you would imagine, would not taste very nice at all. It would be extremely heavy and filling and would most probably fall to the pit of your stomach – like a rock – AND it had rocks in it too! Experts have found small pieces of grit in samples of this bread taken from old Viking settlements in York.

VICIOUS VIKING ANCIENT JOKE

VICIOUS VIKING HISTORIANS

We have learned a lot about the Vikings from the people who wrote histories of Britain many years ago. The trouble is that the writers often gave their opinions, which is not the same as giving us *facts*.

WHAT THEY SAID ABOUT THE VIKINGS...

For nearly 350 years we and our forebears have lived in this most lovely land. Never before has such a terror appeared in Britain as we have now suffered from this pagan race. No one thought such an attack could come from the sea.

Alcuin 735-804 AD

- a monk and a very bad loser

The town of Hedeby (in Denmark) is poor in goods and wealth. The people's chief food is fish because there is so much of it. If a child is born there it is thrown into the sea to save bringing it up. I have never heard anything more horrible than their singing. It is more like the barking of dogs only twice as beastly.

Al-Tartushi

- an Arab trader and a bit of a snob

...AND WHAT THEY DIDN'T SAY!

> *A furore Normannorum, libera nos Domine.*
> *(From the fury of the Northmen, deliver us, O Lord.)*

This is what the poor English were *supposed* to have chanted as they trembled in their tiny churches. Nearly every book on the Vikings quotes this prayer of terrified people. The truth is there is no evidence that anyone ever actually said these words! It's simply something that scholars and teachers think they should have said.

TOP FIVE VIKING HITS

- **SING US A SAGA**
- **PILLAGE IN THE VILLAGE**
- **NO SLEEP 'TIL VALHALLA**

THOR'S HAMMER
(SWING MIX)

- **LOKI HOKEY POKEY**

WHAT THE VIKINGS DID DO...

There is a story that King Canute (or Knut) sat at the edge of the sea and tried to tell the tide to go back, saying "I command you not to rise over my land and not to wet the clothes or feet of your lord!" The tide came in anyway and soaked him.

The story is true. Teachers used to tell it to children and say, "What a foolish man King Canute was, children!"

BUT they forgot to say that the story went on – King Knut jumped back on dry land and said, "Let it be known to all people that the power of kings is empty and weak. Only one person is fit to be called king. That is the Lord God who is obeyed by heaven, by earth and by the sea!"

Knut took his golden crown off and never wore it again. He wasn't saying, "Look how great I am." He was saying, "Look how weak we are compared to God."

125

...AND WHAT THEY DIDN'T DO!

Samuel Pepys wrote in his diary of 10 April 1661 that he went

> to Rochester and saw the cathedral where the great doors of the church are, they say, covered with the skins of the Danes.

This was said to be the fate of invaders who were caught – skinned alive in revenge and the skin nailed to the church door. But tests on a "Daneskin" at Westminster Abbey proved it to be the skin of a cow!

True or false...?

1 There was a rule to stop Vikings fighting each other on the longboats.

2 King Alfred had a beard.

3 The Viking men and women wore make-up.

4 King Alfred's wife claimed that the god, Odin, was her ancestor.

5 Viking Halfdan was so wicked that God turned him mad and made him smell so rotten that no one would go near him.

6 The Viking longboats were as long as a tennis court.

7 A longboat sail could cover a tennis court.

8 The Saxon cure for losing your voice was to make the sign of the cross under your tongue.

9 Alfred the Great didn't build many monasteries because they were favourite targets of the Vikings.

10 Viking longboats had no seats.

ROTTEN RIDDLE

HOW DID THE VIKINGS SIGNAL FROM SHIP TO SHIP?

THEY USED NORSE CODE

BOK

Answers:

1 True **2** False **3** True **4** True **5** True (According to the monk, Simeon of Durham) **6** True **7** False (It would take three sails to cover a tennis court) **8** True **9** True **10** True (The oarsman sat on the chests that carried their belongings)

THE SAVAGE SAXONS

The Vikings may have been called vicious but we have to remember they lived in harsh times. Their enemies in the British Isles, the Saxons, weren't far behind when it came to being cruel.

At least two English princes killed their brothers to win the throne of England: Harold Godwinsson did it through battle and Ethelred did it through murder. And they weren't the worst!

SIX SAVAGE SAXON STORIES

1 King Edmund Ironside was a fierce fighter. In one battle, an enemy called Edric climbed a hill and waved a severed head in the air. "Surrender!" he called to Edmund's men. "This is the head of your leader, Edmund!"

Edmund was furious. He tore off his helmet to show his men that he was still alive. He then flung his spear at Edric. He threw it so hard that it bounced off Edric's shield and went through TWO soldiers who were standing beside him!

2 Edric's son finished Edmund off in the nastiest way you could imagine. One night Edmund went to a room with a pit that was used for a toilet. In the darkness he didn't see Edric's son hiding in the pit. As King Edmund sat down on the toilet the young man struck him twice from beneath with a dagger ... ouch!

But the Viking King Knut was not amused by this cheating. When Edric went to tell Knut he'd got rid of the Vikings' greatest enemy he promised to reward Edric. "I will place you higher than any other English noble." He did. He cut off Edric's head and stuck it on the highest battlement of the Tower of London!

3 Earl Godwin was banished from England for disobeying the good King Edward. A year later Godwin returned. He went to dinner with the king and tried to be a bit of a creep. "People say I killed your brother," he told the king. "But, if that is true, then may God let this piece of bread choke me." A minute later Godwin was dead. He had choked on the piece of bread!

4 The Saxons were Christians and when they defeated the Vikings in battle they often made the Vikings become Christian. But Christianity at that time wasn't all sweetness and light! Early in the tenth century AD, Pope Stephen VI was elected as head of the Catholic Church in Rome. One of his first acts was to put the previous Pope, Formosus, on trial for dishonesty and evil living. Formosus was found guilty because he refused to plead when asked, "Are you guilty or not guilty?" Of course the reason he didn't plead was that he was dead at the time; Stephen VI had had him dug up and his body brought to court. The guilty corpse was thrown into the River Tiber. (You'll be pleased to hear that gruesome Stephen VI died soon after – imprisoned then strangled in his cell.) And they called the Vikings savages!

5 The Vikings attacked the north-east coast of England and its monasteries in 793 AD. Then, as your teacher and your timeline will tell you, they didn't bother much for another 40 years! Why not? The truth is too horrible for school books to tell you ... but this **Horrible History** will tell you! After the 793 raid on Lindisfarne, the Vikings came back to attack the Jarrow monastery on the River Tyne. But this time bad weather held up their landing. By the time they reached the shore the local people were armed and ready. The Vikings landed – and were attacked fiercely. The Viking king was captured and tortured to death. The bloody remains were sent back to Denmark as a warning of what would happen if they tried to attack again!

So the Vikings missed out England for 40 years …
and went round to pillage Ireland instead!

6 The Saxons didn't like Abbot John of Athelney,
even though he was King Alfred's choice. Abbot
John was a German who was very harsh with the
people who visited his churches. So the local people
planned to kill him and dump his body outside the
house of a woman. (They wanted it to look as if he
was visiting her when he was killed by a jealous
lover.) But the plot went wrong. The big abbot
fought for his life. He was cut on the head but his
cries brought help to rescue him.

EDMUND'S EVIL END

If King Edmund's serving girls could write, and
if one of them had kept a diary, then some of it
might have looked like this…

ETHEL'S DIARY

27 May 946

Dear Diary,

That's it. I am packing this rotten job in. My mum wanted me to be a servant to the King. "A great honour," she said. "You start tomorrow!"

"That Edmund's a terrible man for chasing girls!" I told her. "Everybody's heard the story about him and that nun."

"Wulfhilda?" said Mum.

"That's the one. Had her taken to a convent in Hampshire so he could chat her up, didn't he?" I said.

"But he didn't," my mum pointed out.

"Only because she climbed down the convent drainpipes to escape! I don't want to go getting chased down drainpipes," I sniffed.

NOW WHERE'S SHE GONE?

Mum sighed. "King Edmund only chases after pretty girls. You'll be alright."

"Thanks mum," I snapped.

And mum went on to tell me about how to serve and clean and curtsey. She warned me not to spit or swear.

But she didn't warn me about the mess!

I mean to say, it's bad enough normally. All that feasting and throwing bones on the floor. And that bad-tempered King Edmund ordering you about. But last night was the end ... the end for Edmund and for me.

Blood all over the place!

It all started all right. These parties always do. The feast of St Augustine, of course, but that was just the excuse for a booze-up.

I was rushed off me feet all night. I didn't mind too much. They were good lads, mostly, as long as I kept their mead cups full. But there was one I didn't like the look of at all. Dirty hair over a low forehead and a scowl that could kill a cat.

Suddenly the King looks at this villain. He jumps to his feet and shouts, "Leofa!"

The ugly man rose to his feet and sneered. "That's me!"

"I banished you for thieving six years ago!"
the King cried and rushed forward. He grabbed
this Leofa by the hair – personally, I don't know
how he could bear to touch that filthy mop. But
he did, and he threw the robber on to the floor.

Now everyone gathered round in a circle and
started shouting. You know the kind of thing,
"Get stuck in, Eddie! Put the boot in, your
highness!" and so on.

So the two of them are wrestling on the floor
and suddenly the King gives a great cry. He
jerks up and falls back.

I knew at once there was something wrong.
I could tell because there was a long dagger
sticking out of the king's chest.

"Ooooh!" the crowd gasped, as they do. All
I could think was that all that blood would
take a lot of clearing up in the morning.

And somebody yelled, "That's cheating, that
is. Using daggers isn't fighting fair!"

And someone else said, "The King's dead …
there'll be trouble, you mark my words."

Then a man behind me growled. "That's
murder, that is! Get him, lads!"

Now I saw this with my own eyes so I swear
it's true. Nobody used a weapon on Leofa. But

in the flutter of a butterfly's wing Leofa was torn apart. That's right, torn.

It was a nasty death … but a quick one.

It was also a very messy one.

Oh, yes, they took the King's body away to give him a fine funeral. A lot of weeping and moaning and sadness. Very sad, I'm sure. But who gets the nasty job of clearing up that mess?

That's right. Me.

Well, I've had enough.

It might be a great honour to serve the King. But if they're going to go tearing people apart then I'm packing it in.

LOOK WHAT THEY'VE DONE TO MY NICE CLEAN FLOOR

St Dunstan predicted the messy murder of Edmund. In a vision, he saw a devil dancing before him. It's a pity he didn't tell Edmund – the King could have worn his knife-proof vest. At least the nuns of Wessex felt a little safer after Edmund's murder! And young Wulfhilda became a saint.

THE SUFFERING SAXONS

Life in the Dark Ages was tough for the Saxons. They had more problems than simply vicious Viking raids to cope with…

TEST YOUR FRIENDS...

1 Saint Dunstan was on his way to the dying King Eadred when an angel appeared and announced, "Behold! King Eadred is departed in peace." But what did Dunstan's horse do?

a) Learned to speak and said, "Nay! Do not say so!"

b) Ran off and dumped Dunstan on his head

c) Dropped dead with shock at the sight of a dirty great angel

2 The story of the Battle of Hastings is told in pictures on the Bayeux Tapestry. But what exactly is the Bayeux Tapestry?

a) A painting on cloth

b) A tapestry (that's a picture made by weaving threads)

c) An embroidery (a picture made by stitching)

3 The baby Ethelred was taken to church to be christened. The monk, St Dunstan, held the baby over the stone bowl that held the christening water – the font. Suddenly St Dunstan announced, "This is an evil sign! While this baby becomes king there will be death for many Saxons!" But what was the evil sign?

a) Lightning struck the church

b) Baby Ethelred cried all the way through the service

c) Baby Ethelred had a pee in the font

4 The Viking King Knut had a son who became king. His name was Harold Harefoot. A Saxon prince, Alfred, came to England to visit his mother. Harold Harefoot was worried that Alfred might try to take over the throne. What did horrible Harold do to Alfred's friends?
a) Locked them up in chains
b) Sold them as slaves
c) Scalped them

5 What did Harold do to Alfred himself?
a) Had his eyes put out
b) Made him promise not to lead a rebellion
c) Gave him money to go away

6 Harold Harefoot died in 1040 and his even-horribler-half-brother, Harthacnut, became king. What was his first act as king?
a) He had a statue built to honour his dear, dead brother, Harold
b) He had Harold dug up and buried in a specially built church
c) He had Harold dug up, the head cut off and thrown into the Thames

7 King Harold Godwinsson was killed at the Battle of Hastings in 1066. But how did he die?

a) He was cut down by a knight's sword

b) He was hit in the eye with an arrow

c) He was wounded in the eye with an arrow then killed with a sword

8 King Alfred was buried in Hyde Abbey. But when Henry VIII abolished the abbeys, Alfred's bones were dug up. Eventually they ended up in Winchester Cathedral. What state are they in today?

a) Mixed up with the bones of other dead Saxons

b) Buried in their own grave

c) Cremated and the ashes scattered over the Edington battlefield

9 What cure would a Saxon doctor offer you for a bad stomach?

a) Drink a bowl of cat's milk mixed with a drop of dog's blood

b) Starve until noon, take a hot bath then drink treacle in warm water

c) Two indigestion tablets

10 Three Irish monks fled from the Vikings. They reached England safely. King Alfred saw this as a miracle of God because…

a) They had sailed in a boat made of wickerwork and stretched skins and had no food, no oars and no steering plank

b) They had walked across the Irish Sea at low tide

c) They had stolen a Viking longboat and sailed across the Irish Sea

HERE'S WHY!

1c) And, would you believe it, when Dunstan arrived at the palace, King Eadred was dead! He died at the moment that the angel appeared. (But he might have been able to save the king if his horse hadn't turned up its hooves and made Dunstan late!)

2c) It is a strip of embroidered linen measuring 40 metres by 50 centimetres – it tells the story a bit like a strip cartoon.

3c) Sure enough Ethelred was an unlucky king for the Saxons. Nearly as unlucky as the next baby to be christened in that font!

4a), **b)** and **c)** He also tortured and murdered some.

5a) The blinded Prince Alfred was handed over to a monastery and he spent the rest of his life with the monks.

6c) The dead Harold's head was dragged up in a fisherman's net and buried in the Danes' cemetery in London (St Clement Danes).

7c) That is the way Henry of Huntingdon described Harold's death. Some people have said the Bayeux tapestry shows Harold killed by an arrow, but it's not really clear. Harold's leg was hacked off after he was killed. William the Conqueror was so upset by this disgraceful act that he sacked the knight who did it.

THE WICKED WOMAN OF WESSEX

In the nineteenth and twentieth centuries we've had more years when we were ruled by queens than by kings. But in the 300 years of Viking England there wasn't a single queen to be seen. Saxons reckoned this was because of one woman ruler who'd been so bad they never wanted another.

If there'd been a poet to tell her dreadful story
then the poem would not have sounded like this!
(Only the facts are right!)

Queen Eadburgh and Beothric

King Beothric married a woman, Eadburgh,
A bossy and vicious old crow.
He had a young pal that he liked quite a lot,
Till Eadburgh said, "He'll have to go!"

The King he refused and Eadburgh got cross,
So she poisoned poor Beothric's friend.
Alas for the King he had drunk the same stuff
And came to the same sticky end.

The Saxons they drove out the murdering fiend
And she fled with the loot from their house.
She went overseas to an Emperor's court
'Cos she wanted another rich spouse.

The Emperor said, "You may marry your choice.
Would you prefer me or my son?"
She picked the young prince and that made
the dad mad!
He said, "Right then! You'll get neither one!"

Eadburgh was sent to a convent so quiet,
A house full of nuns good and dear.
But her parties and rave-ups became far too wild
So the nuns threw her out on her ear.

She wandered around with one servant and sank
Down to begging on streets, what a plight!
And that's how Eadburgh came to her sad end.
And the Saxons said, "Serves the bat right!"

KING ALFRED THE CAKE

King Alfred the Great was a winner
A true man of God, not a sinner,
He wrote several books
But wasn't a cook
So don't ask him to look after dinner!

King Alfred is the only king in English history to be called "Great". Just when it looked as if England was going to be overrun by Vikings, he led the resistance and saved at least half of the country.

Like many of the characters who lived in those days, the truth about his life is a little bit mixed up with stories. The trouble is that most of the stories come from a monk called Asser. Asser got his facts from Alfred ... but Alfred could have told a few fibs to make himself look a great hero.
Here are...

TALL STORIES ABOUT ALFRED THE GREAT

How many of these stories do you believe?

STORY 1: Alfred the clever

As a five-year-old boy, Alfie was a bit of a cheat. His mother promised her sons that the first boy who could read her book would be given it. So Alf took it to a teacher. The teacher read it. Alf learned it off by heart, went back to his mum and recited it.

Facts: This is one of Asser's stories. In another part of his book Asser says Alfred couldn't read "until the twelfth year of his age or even more".

STORY 2: Alfred the spy

He was also a bit of a cheat in later years. He dressed up as a minstrel, wandered into the Viking camp and listened to the Viking plans. A few days later he wandered back to the Saxon camp, spilled the beans, and battered the Vikings.

Facts: This is a story first written down 500 years after Alfred died. Would a king really risk his life in this way? The Vikings might not have recognised him as Alf – but they could have executed him anyway as a Saxon spy!

WHO WAS THAT MINSTREL SNOOPING AROUND?

I DON'T CARE, AS LONG AS HE'S GONE... WORST SINGING I EVER HEARD

STORY 3: Alfred the friend of a ghost

Alfred seems to have had a bit of supernatural help. The Saxons claimed that the ghost of St Cuthbert appeared to Alfred and told him how to beat the Vikings! After Alfred died he was buried in the old Hyde abbey until the building of Winchester was finished. Then he was moved. But monks claimed that his ghost stayed and haunted Hyde Abbey!

Facts: Asser said it was St Neot who appeared! But perhaps Asser was trying to show how great the south-of-England Saint, Neot, was. The Cuthbert story was told by a northern monk … trying to prove how powerful the northern St Cuthbert was!

STORY 4: Alfred the inventor 1

Alfred was supposed to have invented the clock! He needed to measure time so he could spend half of each day and night praying. But sundials don't work on cloudy days … and they work even worse at night! So Alfred had candles marked in inches and measured the hours by the time it took to burn. But, in the draughty churches, the candles blew out.
So…

STORY 5: Alfred the inventor 2

Alfred invented the lantern! There was no glass but clever Alf had ox-horn cut so thin that you could see clean through it.

Facts: Both are stories from Asser.

STORY 6: Alfred the inventor 3

Alfred invented the navy. He decided that it was a good idea to attack the Vikings at sea, before they landed. At sea the Vikings were cramped into their longboats and couldn't fight and row at the same time. Great idea ... Alf made it work well.

Facts: The truth is his dad and his grandad both attacked the Vikings at sea as long ago as 851, off the Kent coast.

STORY 7: Alfred the religious

Apart from praying day and night Alfred sent money to the Pope in Rome. In 883 Pope Marinus sent Alfred a present – a lump of wood that was supposed to be from the cross on which Jesus was crucified.

Facts: Marinus died. The next Pope, Formosus, pinched the church's money, and poisoned his brother and his wife. Alfred stopped sending money!

MAYBE IF I SENT ALFRED SOME MORE BITS OF WOOD HE'D START SENDING MONEY AGAIN

STORY 8: Alfred the humble

When Alfred was having a bad time against the Viking invaders he hid out in a forest. A forester's wife gave him the job of watching her cakes to make sure they didn't burn. Alf was so busy fixing his bow that he forgot to turn the cakes over. They burned. The woman gave Alfred a piece of her mind. He could have said, "You can't talk to me like that – I'm the King!" Instead he just said, "Sorry."

Facts: This story is first found written down 400 years after it happened. Another 400 years passed and the Archbishop of Canterbury made a copy of Asser's book ... and slipped the story of the burning cakes in! Other historians copied it, thinking it came from Asser and must be true!

Final Fact: Don't believe everything you read!!!

JUDGE FOR YOURSELF

King Alfred took all the old laws and organised them into a new book of laws for the Saxons. Some of the laws were fair – others were pretty daft.

For example, there were four ways of finding out if a person was guilty of a crime. They were called ordeals. If you passed through the ordeal you were innocent – but if you failed you suffered from both the test and then a punishment.

Imagine you have been accused of a terrible crime – somebody has let your teacher's bicycle tyres down! The finger of suspicion is pointing at you.

"I didn't do it!" you cry.

"I think you did!" the tyreless teacher trembles. "Take a trial by ordeal! If you refuse to take the test then you are guilty – take your pick of ordeals!"

CHOOSE YOUR ORDEAL

1 **Ordeal by cake:** A special cake is baked. Then you must swear:

> *If I did this crime then may this cake choke me!*

and eat the cake.
If you're guilty then you choke on the cake - if you're innocent you live.

2 **Ordeal by cold water:** You are tied hand and foot. A rope is placed around you and you are lowered into a pool. If you sink then you are innocent … and with a bit of luck you'll be hauled out before you drown. If you float then you are guilty. You'll be dragged out and punished. (This silly test was still being used in the seventeenth century to test people accused of being witches!)

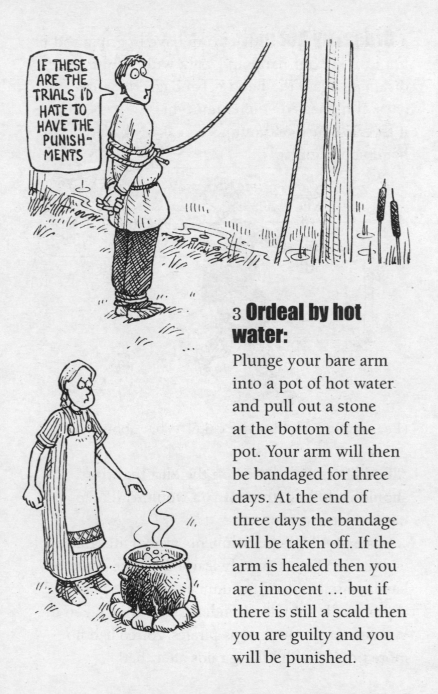

3 **Ordeal by hot water:**

Plunge your bare arm into a pot of hot water and pull out a stone at the bottom of the pot. Your arm will then be bandaged for three days. At the end of three days the bandage will be taken off. If the arm is healed then you are innocent … but if there is still a scald then you are guilty and you will be punished.

157

4 Ordeal by hot metal: You have to grip a rod of hot iron in your hand and walk with it for a set distance. Again the hand is bandaged for three days. If it's healed you're innocent – if there's a burn on your hand you're guilty.

CAN I DO ORDEAL BY COLD WATER NOW?

(Personally I'd go for the cake! What about you?)

Alfred's laws were based on the idea that you shouldn't do something if you wouldn't like to have it done to you.

Some of Alfred's punishments were quite reasonable … but the Vikings quickly learned that he could be harsh on sea-raiders. In summer 896 Alfred's navy captured a lot of Viking raiders. They were taken to Winchester and hanged as pirates. Alfred had no more trouble with Viking raids after that!

Saxon judges were given a clear idea of what punishments to give for crimes. Can you…

MAKE THE PUNISHMENT FIT THE CRIME?

1 The punishment for witchcraft (having dealings with the Devil) was…
a) Having your head shaved
b) Having to go to church every day for a year
c) Death

2 The penalty for plotting against your lord was…
a) Having "traitor" tattooed on your forehead
b) Death
c) Having your toes cut off

3 The penalty for stealing a hive of bees was…
a) A fine
b) To be covered in honey and stung to death by the bees
c) To be covered in honey and thrown into a bear's cage

GAD! I'M BEING LICKED TO DEATH

4 The penalty for killing a man accidentally by letting a tree you are cutting fall on him…
a) You are hung from the tree
b) You are burned on a fire made from the wood of the tree
c) You must give the tree to the family of the dead man

WAIT A MINUTE, THIS CAN'T BE RIGHT

5 The penalty if your dog attacks and kills another person…
a) A fine of six shillings for the first killing, 12 shillings for a second killing and 30 shillings if it kills three people
b) The dog's owner is executed
c) The dog is executed

6 The penalty for telling nasty lies about a person was…
a) Having to walk a mile on your knees to their house and say "Sorry"
b) Having to write a letter of apology and stick it to the church door
c) Having your tongue cut out

7 The fines for beating a freeman, blinding him or cutting his hair were…
a) Ten shillings, twenty shillings and six shillings
b) Twenty shillings, six shillings and ten shillings
c) Six shillings, ten shillings and twenty shillings

8 The fine for accidentally stabbing a man with
your spear depended on...
a) The *angle* the spear
went into him
b) How *deep* the spear
went into him
c) How much blood the
victim lost

9 The penalty for murder was...
a) Hanging
b) Paying a fine to the relatives of the dead person
c) Going to prison for 20 years

10 The fine for offences against women varied.
It depended on how important the woman was.
Generally the fine for an offence against a nun
was...
a) The same as for an offence against an ordinary
woman
b) Half
c) Double

Answers: 1c) 2b) 3a) 4c) 5a) 6c) 7b) That's right. For some
reason it was thought worse to beat him or cut his hair than it
was to blind him! **8a)** The judge hoped that the angle would
show how deliberate the stabbing was! **9b)** The payment to
a victim's relatives was known as wer-gild (blood money).
There were no prisons except in the royal castles. **10c)**

VICIOUS VIKING LAW

I f you didn't like Alfred's Law you could always move over the border into Danish England (Danelaw) and live by their rules. But the Viking Danes could be every bit as brutal as the English...

DANELAW 1:
Sixty sheep to show you're sorry

Eyjolf was clumsy. Probably the clumsiest Viking in town. Tripping over sleeping dogs, dropping his sword on his toe and spilling his mead down his trousers.

"Now look what you've done! Your clumsiness will be the death of you," his wife, Thora, warned him as he crushed a cat beneath his clumsy foot.

"I'm off to the horse fight," Eyjolf muttered, and he snatched up his sword by the wrong end.

"Ouch!" he cried.

"Now look what you've done. Leave it at home," Thora sighed, "or else you'll kill someone."

"A Viking without a sword is like … is like… "

"…is like a Viking with a brain. Very rare," she sniffed and stirred the stew.

Eyjolf barged through the door and there was a splintering of wood. "Now look what you've done! It helps if you lift the latch," Thora snapped.

The man walked carefully down the street and reached the horse-fighting circle without even hurting a single living thing. It was too good to last.

The horse fight was exciting. Hooves flew and men roared. "I've got my money on the black one!" Eyjolf cried as the stallion reared on its hind legs and lashed out with its front ones. "Kill!" Eyjolf shouted. He copied the lashing leg of his horse … and landed a punch clean in the eye of Bjarni the Brutal.

"Ooops! Sorry!" Eyjolf gasped. "Now look what I've done! It was an accident!"

Bjarni's sore eye closed. The other eye looked menacingly at Eyjolf. "You know what this means, Eyjolf!"

"Er … no!" Eyjolf said.

Suddenly the Viking men had lost interest in the fighting horses.

"Kill him, Bjarni!" Ragnar the Ruthless growled.

"Yeah! Chop his clumsy hand off!" someone else put in.

"I've a good mind to," the black-eyed man murmured.

"Oh, come on, Bjarni. It was an accident!" Eyjolf whined.

"It was an insult. And the only way to avenge an insult is to fight to the death! You owe me a debt of honour. I will take your life," Bjarni roared and waved his sword in the air.

"How about if I give you a gift instead?"

"You think you can buy my honour!" Bjarni cried.

"It was just a thought," Eyjolf shrugged.

"How much?" Bjarni demanded.

"Er ... how about thirty sheep?"

"Sixty."

"It's a deal," Eyjolf agreed with a sigh of relief. "I'll deliver them when they're brought in from the hills this autumn."

"I'll come to your farm to pick the best," Bjarni snarled and stamped off over the muddy field.

"That Bjarni's a great fighter," Eyjolf groaned when he reached home. "He'd have killed me Thora!"

His wife scowled at him with a look like a poisoned polar bear. "And perhaps it would be better if he had. We only have sixty-one sheep, you fool. Now look what you've done! We'll have nothing to live on this winter! Go and fetch me the bark off a tree."

"What for?"

"For your dinner. That's all you'll be eating for the next six months!"

And Eyjolf's father, Thormod, was just as bad. "Sixty sheep! Sixty sheep! You must be mad!" he raged that autumn as the sheep were being counted.

"All right, dad, no need to go on about it! Here's Bjarni now, come to collect his payment."

"Here! Bjarni! What sort of Viking do you call yourself? Taking sixty sheep from my son!" Thormod screeched. "You have the guts of a water-weed. What's the matter? Scared in case the clumsy clown beats you? Viking law says clearly that a quarrel must be settled by a fight to the death!"

The furious Bjarni said nothing. He simply turned purple with rage and drew his sword.

"Now look what you've done," Eyjolf grumbled. He drew his sword … and dropped it on his foot. As he bent to pick it up, Bjarni's sword swept down and Eyjolf's head rolled in the mud.

"Now look what you've done," Thora said with a sad shake of the head. "Ah, well, at least honour is satisfied. I guess that means I get to keep the sheep!"

Bjarni turned and walked away without a word. Thormod was speechless. And Eyjolf wasn't saying anything … ever again.

DANELAW 2:
How to finish a fight

Fights were very popular in the courts of
Denmark and Sweden. But if a man was beaten,
and wanted to have his life spared, then he had
to go through a harsh test. This is how to finish
a Viking fight...

1 Play some music on a
fiddle and a drum.

2 Bring a wild cow into the
hall where the fight has
taken place. (Spectators
are often trampled to
death at this point. Try not
to be one of them or you'll
miss all the fun.)

3 All the hair is shaved off the
tail of the wild cow. (This
is an even more dangerous
job than being a spectator –
don't volunteer to do it!)

4 The tail of the wild cow is covered with grease.

5 The victim puts on shoes that are also covered in grease.

6 The victim has to get hold of the wild cow's tail. (And by now it will be really wild – so would you be if someone shaved your tail!)

7 The cow is then lashed with a whip. (Just to make sure it's really, really wild!)

8 If the man can hang on to the cow whilst it charges about the hall he can keep the cow. He can also keep his life.

(**Please note:** It is recommended that you do not try to sort out school-yard fights using this Viking method. The RSPCA would not allow it!)

TEST YOUR TEACHER...

After reading this book you should know a bit more about the Vikings and the Saxons. Now's your chance to shock and amaze the people who thought you were as stupid as you look...

Here's a quiz for anyone who thinks they know anything about Viking times … like a teacher. If they get more than nine out of ten they're doing pretty well.

1 Eilmer was a monk at Malmesbury Abbey and in 1030 went down in history for being the first man to cover 200 metres…
a) Underwater
b) Flying
c) Running in under 25 seconds wearing his habit

2 When a Viking died a long way from home what might his friends do?
a) Bury him where he died
b) Have monks boil his body till there were just bones left and carry them home in a box
c) Cut out his heart and carry that home for burial

CAN'T YOU WAIT TILL I'M DEAD?

3 Why did the god Odin have only one eye?
a) He lost one in a fight with a raven
b) He swapped one for a drink from the well of wisdom
c) He gave one to some starving people to eat – they mixed it with milk to make eyes-cream

4 What was a tree-smith?
a) A carpenter
b) A woodcutter
c) One of the Smith family who lived in a tree-house

5 Vikings used "kennings" or word-play. So a "horse of the waves" was a ship. What was "the sweat of the sword"?

a) Rust

b) Blood

c) The handle where the warrior placed his sweaty hand

6 One Viking called his most prized possession "Leg Biter". But what was "Leg Biter"?

a) His guard dog

b) His sword

c) His pet polar bear

7 Vikings brought a lot of their words to the English language. But what does the place-name, "Follifoot", mean?

a) Stupid place to build a castle (Folly Fort)

b) Place of the horse fight

c) Place where Earl Folli first set foot

8 Did Vikings wear horns on their helmets?

a) Sometimes … for important ceremonies

b) Always

c) Never

FOR HIM TAKING A BATH IS AN IMPORTANT CEREMONY

9 How did the Vikings know which direction to sail in when they were in the middle of an uncharted ocean?
a) They used a compass
b) They threw a raven into the air and saw which way it flew to land

c) They tossed a coin to decide

10 Where did the leader of a longboat crew sleep?
a) At the front of the ship to keep a lookout
b) In the middle of the ship so he was protected by men on all sides
c) At the back of the ship to be near the steersman

HERE'S HOW!

1b) Eilmer attached home-made wings to his arms and jumped off the top of the Abbey tower. After flying nearly 200 metres, the ground broke his fall. And he broke both legs and was crippled for life. He blamed his failure on the lack of a tail.

2b) A Professor Nylen believes that this explains why some graves are found with a jumble of bones rather than with them laid out correctly as if the body had been buried whole.

3b) If your teacher says the answer is **c)** then they're even dafter than they look!

4a) A "smith" was a craftsman. Vikings had weapon-smiths, ship-smiths, jewellery-smiths and so on.

5b) Blood was also known as the "sea of the wound".

6b) Swords were given names such as "Adder" … because its bite could kill. Another was known as "Gleam of Battle". What would you call yours?

10c) The second-in-command slept at the front.

EPILOGUE

Of course, this book has looked at the vicious side of Viking life. Not all the Vikings were vicious … and the ones who *were*, weren't vicious *all* the time. Some people even believe they were rather nice people. Good farmers, clever craftsmen and talented artists.

And some historians even argue that the Vikings were just *misunderstood*.

They never really meant to invade England anyway! An early report of a Viking landing in Wessex describes a landing by just three ships. The local tax collector thought they were trying to do a bit of smuggling so he ordered them to be taken to the castle of the local king.

Afraid of being locked up, when all they wanted was to do a bit of trading, the Vikings killed the tax collector and his men. When they came back next time they brought their mates and decided to really teach those bossy English a lesson. That's how 300 years of misery for the English started.

But the historians who say the Vikings weren't vicious are kidding themselves. What they should say is the Vikings were no more vicious than the rest of the world at that time. Here are two final bits of horrible history. You make up your own mind.

The English king, Ethelred, wanted rid of all the Vikings in England – the farmers and traders who'd settled here, not just the warriors. On 13 November 1002 he ordered that all Danish people should be put to death. Many lost their lives, including

Danish women, who were sometimes buried alive, and children. That was the vicious English for you.

Twelve years later a Viking army took hostages and demanded money and supplies for their men.

The Viking army was driven off by Ethelred's army. As they sailed home they stopped at Sandwich in Kent to drop off those hostages. The hostages were alive … but the Vikings had cut off their ears, their noses and their hands. That was the vicious Vikings. Who was worse? English or Viking?

The English king, Alfred the Great, was a strong and clever ruler who did a lot for the people of this island. But so was the Viking king, Knut the Great!

At 6 p.m. on Saturday 14 October 1066, the grandson of a Viking, King Harold Godwinsson, died at the Battle of Hastings. He was cut down by the sword of a Norman knight.

The Viking age was ended and the last Viking king was gone ... or was he? Because, in a roundabout way, the vicious Vikings won in the end. First they conquered northern France, where a Viking was known as a North Man – or "Norman". Then the "Norman" William The Conqueror invaded Britain and won. So, if Normans are Vikings, then Vikings conquered England!

Nobody has ever invaded and conquered Britain since. If your family has lived in Britain since those times, it's certain that you have some Viking blood in you! Perhaps you may find out the next time you go to the zoo. If you find yourself looking at the polar bears, and feeling a strange urge to eat one...

LOOK WHAT I GOT FROM THOSE FUNNY NORMANS

GRISLY QUIZ

QUIZ

NOW FIND OUT IF YOU'RE A VICIOUS VIKING EXPERT

QUICK VIKING QUESTIONS

1 The Danish Vikings had been invading England for centuries and some had settled – but they weren't popular. In 1002 the good folk of Oxford found a way to deal with the Danes who'd settled there. What way? (Clue: they liked to chop and change)

2 In 1004 the people of Norwich made a deal with the Vikings to stop the raids. What did they agree? (Clue: crime pays)

3 In 1006 King Ethelred of England was worried that his nobles were becoming too powerful. He had one noble, Aelfhelm of York, murdered. What did he do to make sure Aelfhelm's sons didn't rise up in revenge? (Clue: they didn't see the point)

4 By 1009 King Ethelred was desperate. He had paid fortunes to the Danes and they still raided and robbed England. What did he order his people to do? (Clue: oh my God!)

5 In 1010 a medical book of cures was printed, but not many people could read. They preferred old charms like 'Out little spear if you are in here.' What does that cure? (Clue: saves nine)

6 In 1014 Danish King Knut invaded Lincolnshire and took hostages. But when he was driven out by the English he didn't kill the hostages. What did he do? (Clue: a bit of this, a bit of that)

7 The Archbishop of Canterbury was captured by the Danes in 1012. He refused to pay a ransom so the drunken Danes pelted him with what? (Clue: they were feasting at the time)

8 Ethelred died in 1016 and councillors in Southampton elected Danish Knut king – while councillors in London elected English Edmund. Two kings for one kingdom? But Edmund came up with an easy solution. What? (Clue: dead easy in fact)

9 Knut became King of England in 1017. What did he do to the mother of his rival, Edmund? (Clue: knot a bad idea)

10 Eilmer the Monk broke both his legs in 1030. What was the mad man of God trying to do? (Clue: pigs might)

11 In 1040 Macbeth became King in Scotland. How did he kill the previous king, Duncan? (Clue: all's fair in love and…)

12 King Harthacnut accepted a drink from his half-brother and died in 1042. What sort of drink killed him? (Clue: half-brother gets the throne)

13 In 1054 King Macbeth of Scotland was beaten at the battle of Dunsinane. How long did he go on reigning after the defeat? (Clue: count Shakespeare's witches)

NAME THAT NORSEMAN

The people of the eleventh century were often named after their appearance. These nicknames were usually invented long after the person died by medieval writers. (It probably would have been a bad idea to go up to a Viking and call him 'Mr Flatnose'.)

THERE GOES KEITH-REALLY-QUITE-A-NICE-NOSE-WHEN-YOU-LOOK-CLOSELY

Can you spot the real names here?

1 Viking Chief, Thorkell the…
a) Tall **b)** Thin **c)** Thick-as-Two-Short Planks

2 Danish conqueror, Svein…
a) Fork-tongue **b)** Forkbeard **c)** Fork-and-knife

3 Ethelred's son, Edmund…
a) Ironheart **b)** Ironside **c)** Iron-me-shirt

4 Strathclyde king, Owen the…
a) Bald **b)** Hairy **c)** Permed

5 King Knut's son, Harold…
a) Flatfoot **b)** Harefoot **c)** Five-foot-two

6 Earl of Orkney, Sigurd the…
a) Stout **b)** Slim **c)** Stuffed

7 Archbishop of York, Wulfstan the…
a) Wolf **b)** Fox **c)** Yeti

8 Duke of Normandy, Robert the…
a) Saint **b)** Devil **c)** Slightly Naughty

9 Norse king of the Irish, Sigtrygg…
a) Silkbeard **b)** Squarebeard **c)** Bottle o' Beard

10 Wife of King Harold, Edith…
a) Swantail **b)** Swan-neck **c)** Swansbum

11 King of Norway, Magnus…
a) Barefoot **b)** Bareback **c)** Bear-hug

POTTY PROVERBS

The armies that invaded England brought with them terror, destruction, fear and … language! The Viking invaders brought many words that we still use today.

These incredibly intelligent words of wisdom would not be possible if it hadn't been for the kindly Viking conquerors. Can you spot the *three* Viking words in each of these little-known Norse proverbs?

1 A flat egg on the plate is worth two in the dirt.

2 Bulls without legs give fewer steaks to the butcher.

3 Grubby kids with freckles don't look so mucky as those with plain faces.

4 Thieves who crawl low are not seen from high windows.

5 Reindeer with scabs give rotten meat to stew at Saturday suppers.

6 Dirty fellows become dazzling when washed with soft soap.

7 A knife in the guts will get even the grandest to gasp.

8 A score of scowling scarecrows will scare scamps.

9 Those who die meekly will receive no glittering crown in heaven.

10 Walk awkwardly and cruel people will scream and call you lame.

ANSWERS

QUICK VIKING QUESTIONS

1 The Danish men, women and children in Oxford were massacred. The English chopped them to bits or fried them alive in a church like Danish bacon!

2 The people of Norwich paid 'peace money' – a bribe. Of course the Vikings took the money and then robbed and destroyed Norwich anyway! Wouldn't you?

3 Ethelred had them blinded. Nasty.

4 Pray. King Ethelred ordered everyone to go barefoot to church and eat nothing but bread, water and herbs for three days. He also ordered them to pay taxes or be punished.

5 A stitch.

6 He cut bits off them – noses, ears, fingers, hands and so on. Nothing too serious.

7 Cattle bones. He was probably stunned and didn't feel the killer blow – with an axe. Dane leader Thorkeld was disgusted by the murder. Even Vikings have feelings.

8 Edmund died. Knut became king of all England.

9 He married her.

10 Fly. He stood on a tower with wings strapped to his arms, waited for a strong gust of wind, then he jumped and flapped. He got 200 metres before he crashed.

11 In battle. Forget William Shakespeare's play where Macbeth stabs Duncan in his bed – Macbeth won fair and square.

12 A poisoned one. This murder was never proved but no one was bothered one way or the other. No one liked Harthacnut anyway.

13 Three years. Shakespeare got it wrong again! In his play (with three witches) Macbeth is killed at the battle of Dunsinane.

NAME THAT NORSEMAN

1a 2b 3b 4a 5a 6a 7b 8b 9a 10b 11a

Please note: anyone who answered (c) for any question may need a brain implant.

POTTY PROVERBS

1 Flat, Egg, Dirt
2 Bulls, Legs, Steaks
3 Kids, Freckles, Mucky
4 Crawl, Low, Windows
5 Reindeer, Scabs, Rotten
6 Dirty, Fellows, Dazzling
7 Knife, Get, Gasp
8 Score, Scowling, Scare
9 Die, Meekly, Glittering
10 Akwardly, Scream, Call

INTERESTING INDEX

Where will you find 'cattle-droppings', 'giants' armpits' and 'horse-fights' in an index?

193

TERRY DEARY

Terry Deary was born at a very early age, so long ago he can't remember. But his mother, who was there at the time, says he was born in Sunderland, north-east England, in 1946 – so it's not true that he writes all *Horrible Histories* from memory. At school he was a horrible child only interested in playing football and giving teachers a hard time. His history lessons were so boring and so badly taught, that he learned to loathe the subject. *Horrible Histories* is his revenge.

MARTIN BROWN

Martin Brown was born in Melbourne, on the proper side of the world. Ever since he can remember he's been drawing. His dad used to bring back huge sheets of paper from work and Martin would fill them with doodles and little figures. Then, quite suddenly, with food and water, he grew up, moved to the UK and found work doing what he's always wanted to do: drawing doodles and little figures.

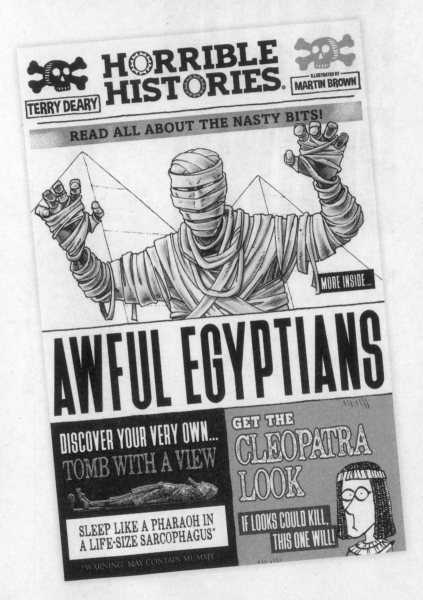

HORRIBLE HISTORIES

TERRY DEARY

ILLUSTRATED BY MARTIN BROWN

READ ALL ABOUT THE NASTY BITS!

ROTTEN ROMANS

NEW SERIES OF GLADIATOR!

- AMPUTATE MANGLED LIMBS
- REMOVE TONSILS
- MEND BROKEN BONES

ROMAN WAITING TIMES DOWN!

BUSTED!

STONE-FACED KILLERS

MORE INSIDE...

HORRIBLE HISTORIES.

TERRY DEARY

ILLUSTRATED BY MARTIN BROWN

READ ALL ABOUT THE NASTY BITS!

MEASLY MIDDLE AGES

MORE INSIDE...

HORRIBLE HISTORIES.

TERRY DEARY

ILLUSTRATED BY
MARTIN BROWN

READ ALL ABOUT THE NASTY BITS!

TERRIFYING TUDORS

MORE INSIDE...

TERRY DEARY

HORRIBLE HISTORIES.

ILLUSTRATED BY
MARTIN BROWN

READ ALL ABOUT THE NASTY BITS!

FRIGHTFUL FIRST WORLD WAR

MORE INSIDE...

● **READER OFFER**
HOUND HELMETS
TOKEN COLLECT

WIN!
A YEAR'S SUPPLY OF LICE SOLUTION FOR ONE LUCKY READER*
*FREE BACK-SCRATCHER FOR TEN RUNNERS-UP!

HORRIBLE HISTORIES

TERRY DEARY

ILLUSTRATED BY **MARTIN BROWN**

READ ALL ABOUT THE NASTY BITS!

WOEFUL SECOND WORLD WAR

TANKS A LOT!

LET'S GET READY TO RUMBLE!

POP!

SPY-EYE!

HAVE YOU GOT WHAT IT TAKES?

MORE INSIDE...

HORRIBLE HISTORIES.

TERRY DEARY

ILLUSTRATED BY
MARTIN BROWN

READ ALL ABOUT THE NASTY BITS!

UP IN THE AIR

LEGENDARY LEAPERS

**PARACHUTE
DESIGN
FALLS FLAT**

THE WRIGHT
(and wrong) WAY TO FLY

MAD DASH ENDS IN CRASH

**AMELIA'S
AIR** ♥

OOPS, THAT'S BLOWN IT!

**WHAT
GOES
UP
MUST
COME
DOWN**

EEK!

MORE INSIDE...